Once Upon A Dream

Poets From Nottinghamshire

Edited By Sarah Washer

First published in Great Britain in 2017 by:

YoungWriters
Est. 1991

Coltsfoot Drive
Peterborough
PE2 9BF
Telephone: 01733 890066
Website: www.youngwriters.co.uk

All Rights Reserved
Book Design by Spencer Hart
© Copyright Contributors 2016
SB ISBN 978-1-78624-823-7
Printed and bound in the UK by BookPrintingUK
Website: www.bookprintinguk.com
YB0301C

FOREWORD

Welcome, Reader, to 'Once Upon A Dream – Poets From Nottinghamshire'.

Do you dare to dream?

For Young Writers' latest poetry competition, we asked our writers to dig deep into their imagination and create a poem that paints a picture of what they dream of.

The result is this collection of fantastic poetic verse that covers a whole host of different topics. Snuggle up all comfy and let your mind fly away with the fairies to explore the sweet joy of candy lands, escape creepy nightmares, go topsy-turvy in upside-down worlds, and even join in with a game of fantasy sport. From the weird to the wonderful, this collection has a poem to suit everyone.

Whereas the majority of our writers chose to stick to a free verse style, others gave themselves the challenge of other techniques such as acrostics and rhyming couplets.
There was a great response to this competition which is always nice to see, and the standard of entries was excellent. Therefore I'd like to say congratulations to the winner in this book, *Ben Harcourt*, for their amazing poem and a big thank you to everyone else who entered.

I hope you enjoy reading these poems as much as I did.

Keep writing!

Sarah Washer

CONTENTS

Winner:

Ben Harcourt (9) - Nottingham High Infant & Junior School, Nottingham — 1

Church Vale Primary School, Mansfield

Ty Stephen Richardson (10)	4
Oliver Oldham (10)	5
Archie Darby-Stuart (7) & Lilly-Anna Aline Robinson (7)	6
Ella Storey (8) & Jamie Cooper (7)	7
Lucy Roberts (8)	8
Alise Barovska (7)	9
Lesedi Siziba (9)	10
Megan Rose Bingley (7) & Jayden	11
Matilda Rose Carr-Field (9)	12
Jayden Spencer (8)	13
Blaze Poulter (9)	14
Talia Cotton (8)	15
Poppy Birch (8)	16
Sophie Gregory (8)	17
Jamie-Leigh Chadburn (9)	18
Caitlin Richardson (7)	19
Taylor Grace McCormack (8)	20
Ella Fleming (7)	21
Ellis Galaxy (7)	22
Emma Parker (8)	23
William Harris (7)	24
Jessica Taylor (7)	25
Laila Jane West (7) & Archie Thomas (7)	26
Bliss Harriet (7)	27
Sophie Mia Hill (8)	28
Lennon Johnson-Clay (11)	29
S Cooper (8)	30
Kaitlyn Storey (9)	31
Sam Walters (8)	32
William Lean (9)	33
Jordan Dee White (7) & Lexie Bates (8)	34
William Brazier (7)	35
Summer Chadburn (8)	36
Michael Loates (10)	37
Bobby Maddison (8)	38
Freya Grace Housley Wass (8)	39
Louie Maddison (8)	40
Kempton Pothecary (8)	41
Alex Kestle (7)	42
Bailey Pearson (9)	43
Tia Robinson (8)	44

Nottingham High Infant & Junior School, Nottingham

Nikhil Sanghera (9)	45
Rohan Banerjea (10)	46
Otto Greenwood (11)	49
Jake Greenhalgh (10)	50
Azaan Mahmood (10)	53
Sarah Jane Whittamore (10)	54
Ujesh Mahendra Kumar Sakariya (10)	56
Omar Amsha (9)	59
Ayaan Patel (8)	60
Krrish Mehrotra (10)	62
Vuyo Eli Mukange (10)	64
Jai Raj Sharma (10)	66
Alex Barish (9)	68

Name	Page	Name	Page
Louis Jackson (10)	70	Thales Iliadis (10)	124
William Wastell (10)	72	Max Morgan (7)	125
Rayan Navya Kapur (11)	74	Jack Aram (7)	126
Naveen Bala (11)	76	Leon Elliss (10)	127
Luca Vergari (10)	78	Ethan Pickering (9)	128
Mohammed Rayan Mahmood (10)	80	Georgia Grace Aram (7)	129
		Eron Singh Dhami (7)	130
Verroshan Athavan (8)	82	Ruben Evans (8)	131
Noah Bhatia (11)	84	Taran Sabarinathan (8)	132
Thomas Bavin (11)	86	Maxwell Cooper (7)	133
Hukam Singh Sethi (7)	88	Samuel Grayton (8)	134
Saahat Satyam (10)	90	Lohit Deepak (10)	135
Matthew Bancroft (10)	91	Nathan Sood-Patel (8)	136
Finlay Cullen Draper	92	Kitty Strudwick (7)	137
Zayan Baig (10)	93	Ben Massey (8)	138
Seth Dineen (9)	94	Jacob Thomas (8)	139
Roman Elliss (7)	96	Joshua Parsons (8)	140
Zain Khan (10)	97	Sasmeet Satyam (8)	141
Gabe Edwards (11)	98	James Freeston (8)	142
Saketh Chinta (8)	100	Harry Elwick (9)	143
Shuban Yadavakrishnan (9)	101	Sam Grady (8)	144
Benjamin Chadwick (8)	102	Ayotunde Adewoye (8)	145
Yusuf Butt (9)	104	James Bowden (9)	146
Ishan Feroz (10)	105	Kapil Krishanand (9)	147
Jagpal Singh (10)	106	Oscar Armson (7)	148
Ben French (9)	107	Nico Bains (7)	149
Alec Sehat (9)	108	Mandip Singh Leihal (10)	150
Toyan Garland (10)	109	George Thompson (9)	151
Esme Winter (9)	110	Taylor Bradley (10)	152
Jack Battisti Downey (10)	111	Euan Dodd (8)	153
Robert James Henry Goodwin (11)	112	George Akins (8)	154
		Nathan Samuel (8)	155
William Oliver James Harwood (9)	113	Umair Hurairah Nazir (7)	156
		Ryan Mannion (9)	157
Namit Batra (9)	114	Anna Ratan (8)	158
Harry Goonan (9)	115	James Black (10)	159
Nathan Chadwick (11)	116	Rishi Gouni (7)	160
James Golding (7)	117	Edward Mellors (7)	161
Om Kamath (7)	118	Marley Parejo (8)	162
Matthew Moran (8)	119	Alfie Armstrong (7)	163
Aarush Anand (7)	120	Ollie Hustwayte (9)	164
Henry Strudwick (8)	121	Oscar G C Gisborne (7)	165
Isak Ibrahim (11)	122	Nihal Singh (7)	166
Aditya Puri (8)	123		

Farris Hameed (7)	167
Alfie Cooper (8)	168
Josiah Ibrahim (9)	169
Ethan Corne (8)	170
Oliver James Hetfield (11)	171
Fletcher Phoenix (8)	172
George Emerson (9)	173
Alfie Armson (9)	174
George William Turton (8)	175
Michael James Syme-Grant (10)	176
Muhammad Masoom (9)	177
Isa Saleem-Khan (8)	178
Joshua Maida (9)	179
Phoebe Forward (9)	180
Shlok Sahu Bhansali (9)	181
Isaac White (9)	182

St Peter's Academy, Nottingham

Caleb Cope (7)	183
Oliver Joseph Sherwood (9)	184
Lucy Tomlinson (9)	186
Phoebe Tomlinson (10)	187
Yasmin Lyon (9)	188
Evie McDowell (7)	189
Ellie Rimmington (7)	190
Amelia Taylor (9)	191
Amy Clayton (7)	192
Charlotte King (9)	193
Oscar Middleton (9)	194
Edward Paling (9)	195
Max Widdowson (9)	196
Archie William Lever (10)	197
Oliver Henshaw (7)	198
George Kennington (9)	199

Whitemoor Academy, Nottingham

Mustafa Khan (9)	200
Dominic Curtis (10)	202
Niamh Pearce (11)	203
Hugo Kali (8)	204
Jaylah Clarke (8)	205
Christine Rutendo Simbi (8)	206

Willow Brook Primary School, Nottingham

Sami Rahman (8)	207
Lilian Robertson (7)	208
Rebecca Grace Barks (7)	209
Katie Limon (8)	210
Holly Limon (8)	211
Maisy Gallacher (7)	212
Grace Smithies (7)	213
Keira Cullis (9)	214
Harry Whiteley (7)	215
Charlotte Lucy Mutton (7)	216
Ellie Reast (7)	217
Grace Deuchars (7)	218
Bertie George Freestone (7)	219
Izzy Whiteley (7)	220
Ollie Holland (7)	221

THE POEMS

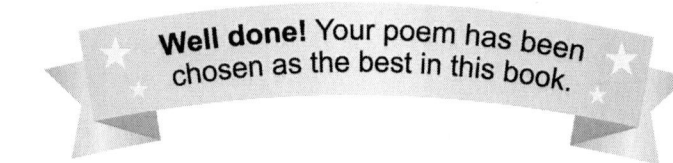

Well done! Your poem has been chosen as the best in this book.

A Boy's Dream

I sailed far from here
With biscuits and beer
And a parrot as my friend
A trusty crew
Some rum and a brew
An adventure that never will end

Meteors whizz by
As I speed through the sky
With asteroids on my tail
Aliens from Mars
With guns full of stars
Shoot my rocket, but I will not fail

A long jungle trek
Quicksand up to my neck
As I grab out and pull on a vine
The monkeys will chatter
As they get even fatter
Eating supper, I hope it's not mine!

A medieval knight
Getting into a fight
With a dragon as fierce as my mum
A princess locked up
In a castle high up
Waiting for her rescuer to come

Monsters with claws
Behind all the doors
Long for a midnight feast
There is nowhere to run
Scream for help but there's none
They are big, brawny, blundering beasts

Cracking a code
Driving fast down the road
To my secret agent base
Bad guys chase behind
They are not very kind
This will be an exciting case

Pyramids rise
Like great towers in the skies
And supreme pharaohs charge out to fight
A sarcophagus of gold
Holds mummies of old
In tombs as dark as night

Speeding through the air
No one would to dare
To battle the almighty me
Invisible and strong
It will not be long
Before all the super villains flee

A rock star on stage
The newspaper front page
Boy, I look really cool
And then from the ground
Comes an unwanted sound
'Wake up, it's time for school!'

Ben Harcourt (9)
Nottingham High Infant & Junior School, Nottingham

A Weird Dream And Nightmare!

One day in my circus house
It was my birthday
All my family came
The oven was burping
My mum was making all of us a cup of tea
My tea said, 'Hi'
And it was a nice day
The frying pans were jumping around
Then I saw some creepy clowns
They jumped over the fence and were all trying to break in
And they did
I stopped them and I was as still as ice
They put me as a hostage
My house was sparkly and gold
Plus sweets were on the walls
Then they put me as a hostage, I was terrified
And I started to cry
Plus the creepy clowns caught my family
And I escaped and saved my family
From the creepy clowns
We called the police
And the creepy clowns got arrested, yay!

Ty Stephen Richardson (10)
Church Vale Primary School, Mansfield

The Future

One day in Warsop
One boy was exploring Warsop
His name was Oliver and he found a cave with a portal in it
He was determined to see what was on the other side
The portal was brighter than the sun
That's what worried him
He felt excited to see what was inside
So he bravely took a step in it
And *boom!* He was inside
The cars were running like the Flash to their destination
Everything was made out of glass, fibre glass
But what was that? A rocket zoomed next to him
There were robots inside with him
They needed him
They zoomed to space, there was the moon racing
They needed to destroy it so they did.

Oliver Oldham (10)
Church Vale Primary School, Mansfield

Rocking Wonderland

It's rocking in Wonderland
The trees are rainbow like a parrot and the birds look like guitars
The candy sun sets and it sets rocking music at night

Fireworks crackle from the rainbow trees
And dragons dance in the air upside down
Fireworks shooting out from behind him

When the candy snaps, *snap, snap*
A solar system revolves around the tap dancing dragon
And candy canes dance on a chocolate cake

There is a giant chocolate bar in the ice cream city
And Mr Ice Cream works there
He is a really good man
He smiles at everyone.

Archie Darby-Stuart (7) & Lilly-Anna Aline Robinson (7)
Church Vale Primary School, Mansfield

Sun Land

In Dreamland it is as hot as summer
And it is very yellow
This is massive, there are dog and puppy statues
We stand on the sun
It is very shiny and bright
The sun is too hot
It burns holes in your shoes, it cooks your food for you
There are babies that talk and they jet off with stuff to make a plane
At night the sun lies down onto the floor
At Dreamland you can stay at school for how long you want
At Dreamland you can do anything you would like to do.

Ella Storey (8) & Jamie Cooper (7)
Church Vale Primary School, Mansfield

Imagination Land

It's always sunny in Imagination Land
The clouds are as white as snow
The sun is as bright as a torch
And the moon at night is as warm as a radiator
The cars can fly like a bird
And bees buzz because of the warmness that flies around the town
The houses tower up over the tallest mountains and we have a lot of mountains
The dance club has people cartwheeling out onto the street
The trees have cherries, apples, strawberries, blackberries and oranges on them.

Lucy Roberts (8)
Church Vale Primary School, Mansfield

Cheesy Land

It's cheesy in Dreamland as yummy as cheese and the trees wobble like jelly
The sun dances like a ballerina and sings about a snowflake
The cheese park is full of hot children's cheese
That is everybody's favourite in the whole world
Pop go the bubbles that float all around the town
That's really fun for children
Some cheese is sparkling as sparkly as glitter in the forest called a sparkle gem
And the king and queen live there.

Alise Barovska (7)
Church Vale Primary School, Mansfield

My Footballing Dream

When I grow up I want to be a footballer
It would be nice to be as happy as a jumping hare
I want to be going to tours
Even the Premier League
I want to be a footballer and be as happy as can be
Being a footballer is a great job
People might not agree
I will miss my family
They'd better not get cross for me missing tea
Even if I don't win
I want you all to know you can be anything
All you need to do is believe.

Lesedi Siziba (9)
Church Vale Primary School, Mansfield

Narnia Land

It's adventurous in Narnia
In summer it's as roasting as burning lava
The river runs faster than a tiger

The moon goes to sleep in the daytime and the clever, fascinating animals can talk

The wind whistles like how loud a lion would roar
Crunch! In the freezing ice in the forest, the snow taps on my shoulder and crunches the ground
The snow is as pale as a vampire's face.

Megan Rose Bingley (7) & Jayden
Church Vale Primary School, Mansfield

My Dream

My dream is to tell you about my house
made out of white chocolate,
everlasting gobstoppers
and sweets.
When I slurp my tea
it seems to me
It is rude to slurp.
It was snowing today
and I heard the snow talk to me, it said,
'Come play with me.'
The town is upside-down,
the sky is as green as a big green tree
And the ground is as blue as a glass of water.

Matilda Rose Carr-Field (9)
Church Vale Primary School, Mansfield

Untitled

Jets and Red Arrows fly past as quick as you blink
The raindrops come up from your feet, it is as strange as water going the other way down the stream
The sun shines upwards and feels weird on your feet
Fireworks fire up and make a banging noise
As loud as a lion's roar
The clouds are like stepping stones but are as soft as a sheep's wool
The rainbows are like traffic lights with the order.

Jayden Spencer (8)
Church Vale Primary School, Mansfield

My Future

In my bedroom, surrounded by laptops and cameras
I've finally found my confidence
Now I'm recording
Quick, before I start exploding
I've already got 10,000 views
Now I'm creating a splendid studio
With laptops, monitors and a gaming sign
Now I'm as calm as my sister
Finally I've made loads of videos
Time to make even more videos.

Blaze Poulter (9)
Church Vale Primary School, Mansfield

In Imagination Land

The fireworks bang amongst our feet
And the colours on the rainbow are like traffic lights
Flashing at random times
The soft cotton clouds make your feet tickle
And the moon rests in the air and the stars start to speed past like flying jets
Also the birds start pecking our feet
And it feels like fish nipping your feet
I hope you had a good night's sleep.

Talia Cotton (8)
Church Vale Primary School, Mansfield

My Upside Down Land

And the winter sun that is as bright as a firework
brushes her hair in the morning
While the army of snow comes up to you
The golden ducks relax on their pond
Up in the green-as-a-leaf sky
The drains on the houses go *drip*
On the sky, the clouds are like a pillow to you
The houses on top of you smell like candy but are as
dangerous as a tiger.

Poppy Birch (8)
Church Vale Primary School, Mansfield

Dream Land

Everything is upside down
Rainbows are sparkling at your feet and smiling at you
The sky is as luscious and green as ever can be
Birds are looking curiously at what has happened
Suddenly I hear a big bang
It is fireworks, it really hurts my feet
The clouds tickle my feet when I walk
Everything is different
I love it
But would you?

Sophie Gregory (8)
Church Vale Primary School, Mansfield

My Dream World

I dreamed about getting a guitar ready for when I grow up
So I can start my own rock band
My rabbit moves slow like a star
My dream house has a choco door and candyfloss windows
I have raindrops in a black and white bucket
They make a splashing noise
The sun is sucking up candy rocks
We can't see anything now because it is sundown.

Jamie-Leigh Chadburn (9)
Church Vale Primary School, Mansfield

Pop Star Land

It's colourful in Dream Land
There are lots of colourful lights that shine brightly in your eyes
And make your eyes glitter
They shimmer in the sun
And in the morning the sun sings a beautiful lullaby to wake me up
I don't get angry
It is very, very nice and it sometimes makes me go back to sleep
I sing very nice songs.

Caitlin Richardson (7)
Church Vale Primary School, Mansfield

Upside-Down World

The moon is coming up while the sun is dancing down
in Upside Down Land
The moon has come up while the snow is drifting down
the green sky
They're shining stars that are so bright as well
While the moon is up and the planets gaze at the stars
The world is moving around the moon
There is a bird house in the sky which is strange!

Taylor Grace McCormack (8)
Church Vale Primary School, Mansfield

Crazy Land

The trees crash together and make lots of noise
It has lots of noise like *fizz* and *pop*, *drip* and *slurp*
It is as beautiful as rainbows

It doesn't snow and the sun moves like a glitter ball
On one side it is rainbow but the other side is normal
It is as lovely as a butterfly.

Ella Fleming (7)
Church Vale Primary School, Mansfield

Gingerbread House

I think when I am asleep that I live in a gingerbread house
With glowing solar lights
Window sills are made of Skittles
And if you eat them you will go to prison
With liquorice restraints
They are as black as a black panther
And the only thing you cannot eat is the snow, it trumps
And it is as pale as the clouds.

Ellis Galaxy (7)
Church Vale Primary School, Mansfield

Upside-Down Land

The sun is grinning at your feet
And the kites fly like an elegant bird
Aeroplanes zoom at your feet and eagles don't cross your feet
The moon glitters at your clean feet
The moon is as sparkly as a sparkly birthday card
The bees buzz around your feet all day and night
The flowers dangle from the emerald skies.

Emma Parker (8)
Church Vale Primary School, Mansfield

Aeroplane Land

It's noisy in Dreamland because aeroplanes zoom through the air
As fast as Usain Bolt
Extreme athletes and paralympians jumping and running in the hot sun
Rainbows race Olympians at 12
After, the rainbows eat their lunch
The land shines in the sun like emeralds
Kapow!
What's that?

William Harris (7)
Church Vale Primary School, Mansfield

Chocolate Land

You zoom through the water clouds
Your clouds fill up when it's windy
And money is so cool because you can buy stuff
You have your dinner upside-down in the sky
And the rain is clear
Windows and the ponies are sparkly as a rainbow and colourful as a sweet
The sunlight is bright in Chocolate Land.

Jessica Taylor (7)
Church Vale Primary School, Mansfield

Diamond Land

It's glossy in Dreamland and there's an emerald city
The door is made of smashed diamond
It's as cool as wishes

The brightness of Emerald City smiles at me when I walk past
In Diamond Land there is a golden palace
And everything is either made of gold, emeralds or silver.

Laila Jane West (7) & Archie Thomas (7)
Church Vale Primary School, Mansfield

Ballet Dancing Land

It's noisy in Dreamland
The ballet shoes are as pointed as a pencil
The tap shoes sound like rain tapping on your shoulder
The ballet dancers are as quiet as mice
The music sounds like a violin
The dancers dance smoothly
Ballet dancers twirl like a dandelion twirling through the air.

Bliss Harriet (7)
Church Vale Primary School, Mansfield

The Dreamland Of Fun

Colourful kites whizz by the spectacular green grass
The rainbows stop cars because they are colourful like traffic lights
The sun sits on the green floor and stares at the people as the people walk by
The aeroplanes go past you as quick as a blink
And the thunder goes bang towards the sky.

Sophie Mia Hill (8)
Church Vale Primary School, Mansfield

My Fantasy Future

Surrounded by people I never saw
In a place I've never been before
I can't believe I'm finally here
Also I'm as happy as a deer
After half-time I went to score
So I shot and it went in
And the coach said I'm as good as a bin
Even though I made us win!

Lennon Johnson-Clay (11)
Church Vale Primary School, Mansfield

Untitled

The raindrops make your feet wet and cold
The sun makes your feet hot and dry
The fireworks at night start to hurt your bottom when you sit on the floor
The lightning makes you jump and stings you like a stingray
When it is healing it makes you go purple, all spots of purple.

S Cooper (8)
Church Vale Primary School, Mansfield

The Upside-Down World

Speedily kites zoom around the open sky and planes whizz around
When you walk on the dark sky fireworks bang at your feet
At night you feel bats flying around you
And itchy insects on your shoulder
There is the moon lying down watching people as they go past.

Kaitlyn Storey (9)
Church Vale Primary School, Mansfield

Upside-Down Land

The birds shoot past your feet
They are so fast you blink once and they are gone
They are as fast as a shooting star
The sun burns your feet when you stand on it
It is so bright
When it's dark there's one special star that shines so bright.

Sam Walters (8)
Church Vale Primary School, Mansfield

My Story

I'm at the army finally
The beds are as hard as rocks
The floorboards are squeaking
The food smacks against my plate
Now I'm going to war
I will win
We finally won the war
But in the middle I felt homesick.

William Lean (9)
Church Vale Primary School, Mansfield

Spooky Dreamland

It's spooky in Dreamland and it has ghosts, giants, spiders and skeletons
The bats are flying in the sky behind the spooky house
There are witches inside the terrifying house
The moon is walking in the sky and shining bright.

Jordan Dee White (7) & Lexie Bates (8)
Church Vale Primary School, Mansfield

Power Ranger Land

It's cool in Power Ranger Land
It's full of rainbow Power Rangers
And they are as brave as dinosaurs
There are lots of energems and a huge shaking volcano
The kind dinosaurs help the Power Rangers.

William Brazier (7)
Church Vale Primary School, Mansfield

Untitled

The sun stands on the floor and glares at passers-by
The jets and Red Arrows go past as quick as a blink
When it starts to rain it sprinkles towards the sky from the ground
There's fire and a rainbow in the sky.

Summer Chadburn (8)
Church Vale Primary School, Mansfield

Rugby Poem

I'm on a rugby pitch playing against Castleford Tigers
By half time I'm sweating like a camel in Egypt
When I get home I look at the charity funds on my phone
They are really, really, really high.

Michael Loates (10)
Church Vale Primary School, Mansfield

Untitled

The rain jumps to your feet in excitement
While the sun shines as bright as gold
The rainbow under your feet is like a slide on the park
And the moon is like a spotlight
The clouds zoom across the floor.

Bobby Maddison (8)
Church Vale Primary School, Mansfield

The Dream Land

The moon glares on the lime floor, staring above the night sky
Cars float around in the lovely dark sky
And the jets zoom peacefully past
And the planes go past
Every time you blink a plane goes past.

Freya Grace Housley Wass (8)
Church Vale Primary School, Mansfield

Untitled

The rain jumps to your feet in excitement
While the sun shines as bright as gold
The rainbow under your feet is like a slide at the park
And your shoes will drip but not your clothes.

Louie Maddison (8)
Church Vale Primary School, Mansfield

Dream Land

In Dream Land jets and Spitfires zoom across the sky
Fireworks hit my feet
They hurt my body
The sun stands on the floor and glares at passers-by
Birds are tweeting at my feet.

Kempton Pothecary (8)
Church Vale Primary School, Mansfield

Candy Land

I can see a big lollipop that you can eat
You zoom through water clouds
The sun is brighter than an emerald
It has lots of sweet shops that talk and ask if you want sweets.

Alex Kestle (7)
Church Vale Primary School, Mansfield

Me And My Dream

I saw muck and slugs and sand
I was with my dad and Ryan and my brother
And I was at a motorbike track
I was racing on a motorbike
I felt happy.

Bailey Pearson (9)
Church Vale Primary School, Mansfield

Untitled

The fireworks near your feet fly in the air
The trees wave on the road
The rain drips on the roof
A blue cloud is dripping rain from around the sky.

Tia Robinson (8)
Church Vale Primary School, Mansfield

Dream Land

In Dream Land there are no limits to what you can do
You could fly a plane underground or you could fly
It's an amazing place to be
When I fall asleep I like to turn my bed into a mode of transport
And so far tonight I'm driving a Formula 1 car
As I go zooming past fourth, third, second, first
It's the last straight until I've won
I ran down the last straight and yes I've won
Next I think, *could a chair really play football?*
Then suddenly I find myself watching Chair FC Vs FCB
I can't believe my eyes
1-0 to Chair FC and ten minutes to full-time
The full-time whistle goes, 1-0, what a game!
Afterwards I find in my pocket a golden ticket
Suddenly my jaw drops and I'm like, 'Say what?'
It was the day, when Mr Willy Wonka opened the door
Instead of finding a whole factory full of chocolate inside, I found a lot of fish
After the tour I say, relieved, 'I never want to see another fish ever again.'
Then all out of nowhere, my mum wakes me up
It's another school day, 'Urgh,' I sigh in annoyance
Where do you go and what do you like doing in your dreams?

Nikhil Sanghera (9)
Nottingham High Infant & Junior School, Nottingham

Classroom

Everything in the classroom looks big today
The teacher as big as an elephant
And the pupils are like gorillas
But I'm still the smallest in the classroom

I'm stood on a large, comfy chair
It used to be smaller than me
So did the table - I was taller than the table
For I'm still the smallest in the classroom

I finally climbed up to the table
A green exercise book there I saw
It smelt of dead grass and
I'm still the smallest in the classroom

Now I see I've shrunk to the size of a pen lid
I can't see why this is happening
All I can see is a black marker pen
And I'm still the smallest in the classroom

I boinged to another table
I boinged again - a tray reached out and grabbed me
I boinged again - just in time - up to the teacher's head
And I'm still the smallest in the classroom

The teacher's blazing hair was cooking me
It would make me a sausage in seconds
I was forced to jump off
And I'm still the smallest in the classroom

Ahead was a pencil case green
It smelt like waste mixed with slime
Ink was dripping from gel pens
And I'm still the smallest in the classroom

I crept into the dark bag
And then I smelt another soul
An eight-legged creature crept out from hiding
And I'm still the smallest in the classroom

It puzzled me then, when I heard it talk
How it talked like a tiger giving a growl
I tried talking back, it was offended
And I'm still the smallest in the classroom

Of this I was made to exit immediately
Chased by the monster itself
It gave me a fright - I'm scared of arachnids
And I'm still the smallest in the classroom

The classroom is as big as the ocean
Therefore it is of ease to get lost
One would surely read a map
For I'm still the smallest in the classroom

I want to be my true standing size
Nobody notices me anymore
The playground: a yard of zombies
For I'm still the smallest in the classroom

The teacher - she thinks I am absent
When actually I'm right here
You'd need the eyes of an eagle to find me
For I'm still the smallest in the classroom

Everything in the classroom looked big that day
The teacher as big as an elephant
And the pupils were like gorillas
But I was still the smallest in the classroom.

Rohan Banerjea (10)
Nottingham High Infant & Junior School, Nottingham

Dream Through A Keyhole

Some nights when I've brushed my teeth
I put my tired head upon my pillow
I shut my eyes and think of all the things I've done
I count to ten and wait for sleep to come

Tonight in the distance I hear the music
Bright, bold sounds distantly gathering
Then brass enters confidently and fearlessly
Lastly the strings begin and music fills my head

This night I'm brave and creep out of my bed
Without thinking, my eye raised to the keyhole
And there it is - a world I've never seen before
A glistening, dancing world I feel I want to join

Shadows dancing against the moonlight
Strange, not scary, swaying bodies
Gently waltzing to the orchestra's rhythm
Laughing and singing, although I see no faces

My hand firmly clutches the door handle
Quietly and slowly I twist the brass knob
Ready to join this fascinating night-time world
A place where dreams come true and become real.

Otto Greenwood (11)
Nottingham High Infant & Junior School, Nottingham

The Land Of Ax

It's foggy in the land of Ax
Tall trees were standing tall
Waving their branches around
Looking down on me
The moon was giving me an evil stare

Rohan the elf was clinging on to me
He was shaking so much
His belt came undone
So his trousers fell down

The avenue was like a cave
Vast and dark
The trees leaned over it
As if trying to create an arch or a bridge

At the end of the avenue
There was a lush, green meadow
With flowers dancing around in the wind
And the grass was swaying
From side to side
In the breeze

The pink, fluffy unicorn
With swirls as white as clouds
And a magical rainbow horn

Shining as bright as the sun
Was dancing across the meadow

The green menacing lion
That was standing on its hind legs
Looking around deviously
Scampering across the meadow
Let out a menacing roar
That shook the Earth

The orange, ferocious tiger
With thick, black stripes
And scars across its face
Was jumping and gliding
With outstretched legs
As it sprinted across the meadow
Howling as it went

A purple and black wolf
With drool dripping from its mouth
That was flying around in the sky
Like a rocket
With its ears flapping about in the wind
Let out a massive scream

Rohan started dancing with excitement
Blown away and over the moon
I started singing
With a heart filled of joy

Suddenly my eyes shot open
And everything disappeared
Sitting up in bed
I still had hope
That they are still out there somewhere.

Jake Greenhalgh (10)
Nottingham High Infant & Junior School, Nottingham

Don't Judge A Book By Its Cover

Lying in my bed, tossing and turning
There's a place to go where no one knows
Entering a world of fantasy where I can be me
Stepping into a world of candy
Walking through, I feel anxious, but why this time?
Everything seems to be the same
Miniature chocolate bunnies
The luscious peppermint forest
This overlooked the velvety doughnut mountain
Which had a molten chocolate lava dwelling in it
Then I sighted candyfloss men which were as soft as a baby's bottom
Pop! Pop! the sugar bubbles said, accompanied by Oreo guards
The Skittles rain pranced around
The whistling wind quite flamboyantly
Crash! Bang! Boom!
Everything transformed into Death Valley
The soft doughnuts turned into a volcano
Bunnies into snakes
Skittles into black rain
Oreos into fighting dogs
Candyfloss to ghosts
Then I awake and feel apprehensive, also depressed.

Azaan Mahmood (10)
Nottingham High Infant & Junior School, Nottingham

My Secret Sweetie World

This place was edible and yummy,
Perfect to fill your tummy,
It was me, Aaron, Harry and Fraser.
We were all dressed in blazers,
As the River Choc followed like waves lapping in the ocean.

We spotted a gingerbread castle,
We decided to adventure in there,
What would we find,
Who knows?

My friends and I couldn't contain ourselves any longer,
We had to eat the liquorice ginger home.
Munch, munch, munch.
That's all that you could hear.

But was someone lurking in the castle?
Would we hear them creeping up behind us?
Not over all that munching and crunching!
We were all in our happy world, not a care who's around us.

One by one we were seized,
By one of these muscly guards.
Into a dark room we were taken.

We all felt guilty, except Harry, who was happily staring at her feet.

Cackling, a wizard appeared,
As the wind whistled through our ears.
'Who ate my castle?' bellowed the grisly wizard.
'We did,' squeaked Harry, who had no knowledge of what to say and where!

We were thrown in a cell;
We had four beds, a bucket and a plate of something else!
How would we escape?
Was this our home forever?

That night we hatched a mischievous plan -
Harry was a great digger.
And the floor was only made of dirt;
Silently she dug; carefully we tiptoed out the cell.

Aaron was a master of kung fu,
So he was in charge of killing the guards.
Back we crept out of the door and there we all were -
In my secret sweetie world.

Sarah Jane Whittamore (10)
Nottingham High Infant & Junior School, Nottingham

Rock, Paper, Scissors

Once, in a dream, there was a town,
It was built from paper bricks,
Creases and folds created it,
And people's lives were paper-thin.

Nothing exciting happened,
This town was rather mundane,
People grew bored of paper,
But they didn't want to escape.

Finn grew up in the paper town,
He believed he lived in a perfect place,
He loved every crease and fold,
He cherished every day.

One day a strange man arrived,
He wanted to destroy the town,
He held up an unknown object,
Sharper than any paper cut around.

For this man was genuinely evil,
He wanted to rebel,
He held out an unfriendly object,
He called the object scissors.

The scissors were sharp like a sword,
Pointy like a needle,
He chopped, snipped and cut,
Until half the town was gone.

Everybody was screaming,
Chaos broke out,
Finn decided he was angry,
And he was going to save the town.

A whisper came around of a solution,
Now Finn was told to search,
For an object that was grey and rough,
They called this item a rock.

Finn found this item in an incredible place,
It was where sand met sea,
He picked it up and ran,
He ran straight to his town.

When the evil man saw the rock,
He bent down and apologised,
The rock terrified him,
And his scissors were destroyed.

From this day onwards,
To celebrate the peace of the town,
A game was created by Finn,
He called it 'Rock, Paper, Scissors'.

Ujesh Mahendra Kumar Sakariya (10)
Nottingham High Infant & Junior School, Nottingham

Dreams

A dream is a magical place where you can do or be anything you want
What if dreams were reality and you could go anywhere you want
You could travel in time only using a Lego brick
Or maybe you wanted to be ruler of the universe
I would possibly want all my drawings to come to life when I wanted them to
Perhaps you would like to teleport into your favourite story
What if all school lessons were about time travelling and building a time machine
Your house could be as large as the moon
However, dreams are like days
Sometimes you have bad days
So, if those bad days were dreams
Then it would be like a nightmare
Chaos would be everywhere
You might find that you're being tickled by the Gruffalo
Or maybe the problem is you're being chased by a Norman knight
A dream is a magical place where you can do or be anything you want
But sometimes, they're best in your head.

Omar Amsha (9)
Nottingham High Infant & Junior School, Nottingham

My Winning Dream

I dream to be a world-class football player
Not working in a supermarket pushing a trolley,
I want to be winning the cup, scoring a volley.

I imagine myself running onto the pitch - a lush green
carpet, silver lines marking my territory
Through the tunnel.
The stadium, woah, this is amazing
Thousands of people
I can see the pattern of the seats.
My heart pounds.

The crowd, thundering for Arsenal
A sea of heads; red my team, blue the opposition
My troops: skilled, quick, intelligent, fierce lions
Like dolphins skimming across the pitch.

The ball flying so fast, it's just a blur to the crowd
Me, I have the ball, *boom!* Pass it to Henri, he glides
across the pitch
Whooshing the ball,
Zips to Bergkamp
Alexis flicks it up
I want to score a header but I need to be tall
I jump, like a kangaroo, all my power

Slap - ow, my forehead!
Straight top left-hand corner
The goalkeeper dives right!

'GOOAAALL!' I shout
The crowd explodes with screaming and cheers!
I try to speak but I can't hear myself
I run around the pitch. Celebrating
I feel amazing.
The whistle blows!

My team has worked its hardest
And now it's time for a break with the cup in our fingers!

If I practise my football, I might go far,
Buy a luxury home and a Bentley sports car
I will practise and practise until my dream comes true
And when I am mega rich and famous
I'll still remember you.

Ayaan Patel (8)
Nottingham High Infant & Junior School, Nottingham

Ghost Party

I could hear loud music, from outside
People dancing like mad
My friend has invited me to this party
Don't know what kind of party it was

I stared at the house
It was black and gloomy
I was already scared
But I went in

I pushed the door open
Creak, it went
Even the floorboards made a noise
I looked ahead

It was crazy
Drunk people were dancing around
So drunk, they didn't even notice me
They just kept dancing

Whoosh. Suddenly everyone vanished
Only I was left
It was as empty as a desert
I felt more scared and frightened

I felt like someone would come and grab me
The door of the house closed
I turned around but no one was there
Then something totally unexpected happened

The house talked
I could not believe it
'I shall kill you now!' it shouted
The house was a ghost world

I tried to run
But right that instant something grabbed me
I screamed
But I was taken

With a jolt I woke up
There was nothing there
It was just a dream
I could see I was breathing very heavily

I calmed myself down and went back to sleep.

Krrish Mehrotra (10)
Nottingham High Infant & Junior School, Nottingham

The Dream

I woke up in a cold, desolate place
Outside someone's back garden
The sky was as dark as the colour black
As the lightning shook the tumbled-down house

The rain poured like shattering glass
As the sun turned to black, thick fog
Walking closer to the old house
I noticed its features
Black windows, black bricks and
Black crows flying round the chimneys

As I walked inside the rotten house
The door creaked and I heard growling noises
My heart paced as my hair stood up on end
The house began to laugh as I stood still in my footsteps

I limped up the stairs to see that my ankle had given in
Walking down the corridor I was greeted
By a pale white ghost, then *poof* it disappeared
Gasping in shock, I plodded on with muck all over my hands

Strolling into the master bedroom
I saw a parade of ghosts jumping and jiving to the sound of haunting music

Trembling like an earthquake, I fainted
Only to feel the air of a ghost rising upon me

I woke up in a cold, desolate place
Outside someone's back garden
The sky was as dark as the colour black
As the lightning shook the tumbled-down house.

Vuyo Eli Mukange (10)
Nottingham High Infant & Junior School, Nottingham

I Have A Dream

Moving frantically in my sleep, I dreamt I was on the move
My duvet had taken off into the sky, I had begun to fly
It was a clear morning with a plane passing by
Luckily enough, for me and the plane, it did not rain, as I was high in the sky

Seeing the clouds hugging the sun gently looked amazing
The birds tweeted in the sunlight, sounding like a piece of beautiful music
Though it was cold, the clouds were a fluffy white blanket that kept me warm
Looking down from above, the trees were dots that you could see below
The plane zoomed across the sky, making an impeccably loud sound
I saw the sun rise like flames from a fire
But I wanted to just fly higher!

In the distance I saw a wizard, with a pointed hat, a white beard and a purple cloak
He spoke with a mysterious croak
With his wand he made the sound of a peculiar swish granting me a wish
All of a sudden he disappeared into thin air like a magical trick

I felt myself bounce back down on my bed, it felt like I was on a roller coaster
Instantly I woke up to the sound of my alarm, it was time to wake up!
I had been on an adventure in my sleep.

Jai Raj Sharma (10)
Nottingham High Infant & Junior School, Nottingham

Dreams

As I step in bed
My mum says, 'Have you read?'
Then I say, 'Yes, goodnight.'
Next she replies, 'Don't let the bed bugs bite.'
Drifting off to bed
Is harder than I suspected
Shutting your eyes whilst staring at everything
Little thoughts rushing along your head, anything
Can happen when you're asleep

The house can get burned down
An abnormal creature crawling around with a frown
A valuable object might get taken
Or simply a cake might be in the oven

Suddenly I fall asleep
First I dream of swimming deep
Down to the bottom of the Great Barrier Reef
Then I meet a chief
That teaches mean teachers
To be kinder than peaches

My next dream is training to fly
High in the sky
Then I fall to the ground, my feet frozen stiff
Trying not to fall off the nearby cliff

Until I can't think of any more dreams
So annoyed of dreams, so happy of dreams
Either way, I still want a dream
Hmmm... 'Wake up,' shouted Mum
Morning already, guess the dreams will happen in maths today.

Alex Barish (9)
Nottingham High Infant & Junior School, Nottingham

Under The Sea

Under the sea it is as blue as the sky
The animals dance around and around and
So do I
It is amazing fun under the sea
They're always having parties and
Never leave anyone out
The fish are nice and polite
You'll never not have fun under the sea
I am glad I dream this dream
And you should too
As the sky turns dark nothing changes
Everyone continues
But suddenly I need to go
I am always sad to leave and never am I not
The sky gets darker and darker as my friends look and frown
But suddenly the most horrible things happen
The sharks come out hungry
Almost like a bee with honey or a cat with a mouse
The sharks had a heart of blood and
Devoured anyone who was dancing
They were like a big old slap in the face
As their gills breathed as hard as iron
And teeth were as sharp as knives

The dream gets darker and darker
As soon as they arrive
And the sea is as dark as night leaning on a cliff
To welcome their arrival
No one likes the sharks and
They don't like you
Nothing about sharks is really good
Especially when they smell your blood!

Louis Jackson (10)
Nottingham High Infant & Junior School, Nottingham

Chase

The gloomy trees were staring at me
My skin started to turn white
Something was stalking me in the night
I needed to run, run fast
Because it was coming, coming fast

I dashed into the forest
I stopped when I was safe, or so I thought
The forest was damp and lifeless
Crawling with bugs
I noticed eyeballs in the bushes that wouldn't blink
I would be dead if I didn't think
Rustle! came a noise from behind
It was close, I must be blind
I needed to run, run fast
Because it was coming, coming fast

I ran deeper, deeper still
I couldn't stop, that was my will
Drip, drop went something on my head
It was blood and it was red
I am starting to think that I am dead
I hear the word 'kill' from behind
I needed to run, run fast
Because it was coming, coming fast

I saw the clearing, I saw the light
Though I mustn't stop or it will bite
When I thought I was there
Something behind me had a white head and it was bare
That was the last thing I saw
Do you think this poem was a bit of a bore?

William Wastell (10)
Nottingham High Infant & Junior School, Nottingham

Train To Outer Space

It was a dark, cold winter's night
Everything was pitch-black
And all you could see was the gleaming steam of
The North Star Express
Suddenly millions of woodland creatures and Pokémon
Climbed aboard, showing their tickets to the conductor
Who was a walking talking cat

Inside it was as big as a city, they even had little buggies to help
Bedrooms were like churches
Beds were like rooms
Fridges were like cars
And taps were a floating block of soap and water!

It all looked very small from the outside
But now you know the truth
Anyway, moving on...
The maps showed nine stops
Mars, Saturn, Jupiter
Pong, Lob and Gish
Some naughty, some nice, but all mysterious in a way

As the driver pulled out
One passenger was left out
James!
He jumped on while smoke went into his face
In the few seconds he couldn't see
He heard an echoing voice
James, James, James! James!
He woke up panting, it was nine-thirty five
He was late for school and
He was covered in soot!

Rayan Navya Kapur (11)
Nottingham High Infant & Junior School, Nottingham

The Haunted House

There was once a scary dream with ghosts and monsters in a spooky house
As I stood outside it, furiously one grabbed me in
Then there came a *bing! Bang! Boom!*
So soon I found it scary
Then I was shaking like a drill, *brr*
Because everywhere around me felt like Hell
There also came twenty bats which gave me a jump scare, aah!
So soon I found it scary
The worst thing in the world happened then
Fighting witches and black ghosts awakened
I ran while swords were flying side to side, shiny!
So soon I found it scary
Now I stepped in sand which was very deep
Felt like it was dragging me in
Sinking like a stone I tried to swim up
So soon I found it scary
Finally the scariest monster came
The one with large fangs, dripping blood, scary looks and a sharp nose
A vampire which made me brighten my eyes as light was shining
So soon I found it scary

I was as scared as a cat as the monster came closer
Then it came close enough to suck my heart which it did
Making me wake up and say
'Ah!' I found it scary.

Naveen Bala (11)
Nottingham High Infant & Junior School, Nottingham

Blitz

That moment when your bedroom walls turn to dust
That moment when the comfort of your home is gone
You are surrounded by debris and dried-up blood
That moment you realise you are living your worst nightmare
That moment you know you are in the Blitz

Bang! Bang! is the first thing you hear
You feel your pulse rising
Your adrenaline pumping fiercely through your veins
But then your nose turns to ice, your hands go blue
That moment you realise what the Blitz is really about
War! War!

In a blink of an eye, everything changes
Suddenly the fight for survival begins
The pressure builds up inside you as you remember
That this click of your finger could change everything
In the end it's too much and you back down
You feel like everything is your fault

The enemy closes down on you
Seconds later you find yourself cornered
You're waving that white flag in despair

It's that moment
That moment when you realise how tough and demanding the Blitz really was.

Luca Vergari (10)
Nottingham High Infant & Junior School, Nottingham

Once Upon A Dream

Whoosh!
As the waves roared
The beast rebounding off the boy
As the sea sound whistled into the ear

The liquid ran down the body
Beasts destroyed the body
As fierce as a haunted house
Were the beasts

Scratching was the boy
Crash! Wave after wave
After wave, after wave
Was that the end of life?

Liquid flowing, the boy drowning
The beast poured down the body with waves
As the wind whistled, whistling
Whistling, whistling

The wind was howling
Waves rushing
Beast rebounding
And worst of all
Near the end of life?

Suspense grew
Crash! Thud!
Howling, howling
Howling

Dark and gloomy
Cold and shivering
Dying moments
Guess what?

Argh!
Liquid was washing-up liquid
The waves were only rain
The beast was hailstones
As I looked out the window doing my homework!

Mohammed Rayan Mahmood (10)
Nottingham High Infant & Junior School, Nottingham

Once Upon A Dream

I dreamed a dream in bed last night
Of places most bizarre
I jumped up to the bright, blue sky
And then I flew very far

I flew to Haribo Land
Oh my gosh, so many sweets
I had to take a bite
Oh my gosh, so many treats!

I found an exit to this wonderful land
I went into it and flew down
It felt so horrible and gross
And I saw an ugly clown

I went into Marshmallow Land
And bounced so super far
I felt the wind against me
And saw a marshmallow car

I ended up going through the ground
I tried to get up but I couldn't get out
So sticky and gooey
And then I was thinking of a Brussels sprout!

I went to Snot Land
I saw some snotty cows
I ended up in the water
And then everyone drowned!

Then I teleported to my house
And I was waiting outside my door
My parents opened up the door and said hello
I mean come on, at least we're not poor!

Verroshan Athavan (8)
Nottingham High Infant & Junior School, Nottingham

Magic Land

It is a very wonderful day in Magic Land
My dog Hooty and I were just wandering around
Then Hooty spotted something among the distant trees
It was a Pegasus, we stood in shock
We had never seen an animal like it
It was truly breathtaking

The plants sang as it landed
And it landed with a soft thud
Its wings were as white as snow
And its hooves were black like coal
As it galloped off we decided to follow it
So we both set off to follow it

It seemed to have led up to a completely different part of the land
Where the plants sighed as you arrived
There seemed to be a lot of Cyclops running about

Luckily Hooty protects me
We were all alone
Until we heard a massive bang in the forest
And that is when a Minotaur appeared
It scared Hooty and I

We had no idea what to do
Until the Pegasus arrived
And took us back to the normal land
Finally we were back, safe in the nice part of the land.

Noah Bhatia (11)
Nottingham High Infant & Junior School, Nottingham

The Chocolatey Ship

The boat was drenched in chocolate
The sea was calm and blue
The wind was like a tiger, roaring down
And little Jack Hawkins stood ready, ready for an adventure
Ready to travel the world on an experience called Cadbury Cruises

Finally he set off on his adventure, an adventure he would never forget
The ship gurgled slowly around Africa where Jack was as hot as a volcano

Then slowly around to North and South America where, down by the coast, big penguins waddled
They waddled around and one even got into his boat!
After all that he got to meet Simon Cowell which was amazing

Then as he went through Eastern Asia, the sea was very rough
But he got to meet M S Dhoni and have a cricket experience playing for India

And on his way back he saw a massive blue whale and a dolphin
Finally, when he reached home, he had a huge treat which was 50% of the boat, which meant free chocolate!

Thomas Bavin (11)
Nottingham High Infant & Junior School, Nottingham

Dreams!

I dreamed a dream in bed last night,
of a cloud as white as milk.
In the fluffy cloud I saw,
a house made of candyfloss with a sugar-coated roof.

I dreamed a dream in bed last night,
of a moon as round as a football.
In the silvery moon I saw,
a can of fizzing pop bubbling like mad.

I dreamed a dream in bed last night,
of a bus wobbling like jelly.
In the double decker bus I saw,
a shoe tap tapping on the floor.

I dreamed a dream in bed last night,
of a bee as stripy as a humbug.
In the mint humbug I saw,
cornflakes crunching in my hand.

I dreamed a dream in bed last night,
of my hair as black as a witch's hat.
In the night sky I saw,
the moon dancing with the stars.

I woke up in the morning,
ran down the narrow stairs.
Lying by the fireplace,
were all the things I dreamt of last night!

Hukam Singh Sethi (7)
Nottingham High Infant & Junior School, Nottingham

The Not So Funny Clown!

Where am I, I don't know
Where my dog is, I don't know
The wind is howling
All I can see is black nothing
I am pretty sure it's a mental asylum
For there are rooms, dark, dingy and sullen!

Suddenly I hear a voice from above, speaking gibberish
Adding onto that a loud thud-like sound crashes
Soon a mysterious figure starts walking towards me
The monstrous face, white with different colours
Splashed on his face giving me the shivers

He looked like a clown
And was carrying a sharp axe, with crimson-red blood running down
Walking towards me, the monster split into three
I am surrounded completely
And am imagining my death scene very easily
In my head I am hoping to be saved desperately
My eyes are shut anxiously

Suddenly my alarm goes off, making me jump
I then open my eyes and am happy to see my mum!

Saahat Satyam (10)
Nottingham High Infant & Junior School, Nottingham

Paradise Island

It's amazing out here on this island
Ten miles off the beautiful sandy coast of Spain
The perfectly-formed palm trees curve carefully over my mansion

Rock-solid Haribo sweets stick to the mansion walls like the Velcro on my shoes
A glass roof lets the sun shine brightly down on my bed in the morning
Like a light being switched on
At night-time the stars glisten in the moonlight through the transparent ceiling

My three-storey mansion is a fun place to be due to the dynamic disco floor
A calming chill-out room is perfect for easing stress
There is family fun with the crystal-white balls at the brilliant bowling alley

I'm happy on my perfect island with my robot called Robo the Great
He flies me around if I climb on his back and tell him my destination
I always want to come back to this dream because it is like being in my own happy Heaven.

Matthew Bancroft (10)
Nottingham High Infant & Junior School, Nottingham

Once Upon A Dream

In Dreamland fearsome monsters rule and trembling humans cower in their tiny doll-like houses
The Gretchins are stinky like a group of toads
Moving their rusty, wicked weapons to new forts
While their smashed and defeated castles
Burn brightly like bonfires on a shivery winter's night

Bull-like Minotaurs roaring like mighty waterfalls
March down long, winding streets
And hunt their mice-like prey with their grubby noses

Superior dragons, flying like hawks
Watch it all go by as they return to their gold-laden caves

The king, puny as a butterfly, hides in his lonely castle, shivering like a plate of jelly

In Dreamland fun is always round the corner
And more thrilling adventures await
Like an over-excited puppy
I cannot wait for my next night's sleep.

Finlay Cullen Draper
Nottingham High Infant & Junior School, Nottingham

For Goodness' Sake!

Bolt upright, you sat in your chair
But, phew, you were still the only one there
As you stood up, the floorboards creaked
And as usual, the door squeaked

Your attention was taken by the gross, mouldy wall
You thought of what would happen when they fall
There would be dust everywhere but finally a way out
You knew it wouldn't happen without a doubt

The wind whistled as loud as a megaphone
But the walls didn't fall, they were as hard as bone
You looked over to the wall, that was bare
And all of a sudden a door materialised there

You closed your eyes and shook your head, you were sure you made a mistake
Whoosh! You were back in the real world, your eyes were open, you were wide awake
Sitting there in your comfy, cosy bed
Oh, for goodness' sake.

Zayan Baig (10)
Nottingham High Infant & Junior School, Nottingham

I Have A Dream

I have a dream
That the world was not polluted
Like lungs full of tar
The air would be clearer
Than a fresh mountain stream

I have a dream
That there are no dictators
No leaders of the pack
Not elected by their own ego
No tyrant's regime

I have a dream
There was no poverty
No famine to roam around like a bully
No fight to keep the ones you love alive
No one should live a life so extreme

I have a dream
That no one should get ill
No one will have to surrender to staying at home
Just because a bug you've caught
Nothing should lower your self-esteem

I have a dream
The world was equal
And nothing could stand in its way
Everybody was happy
And worked as an invincible team.

Seth Dineen (9)
Nottingham High Infant & Junior School, Nottingham

The Leprechaun's Gold

I was walking in Sideways Land where every field is a mountain
I climbed the fields like Spider-Man, hunting for gold like we leprechauns do
I saw a colourful moon but it was a sideways rainbow
And I wondered which end the pot of gold would be at
The answer was none!
Where had it gone?
I turned and saw a boy running like the wind
Tap, tap, tap went his shoes
Clink, clink, clink went the gold
I turned to my ogre and shouted, 'Get him!'
The ogre had gravestones for teeth and colossal cucumbers for fingers
With one swoosh of his wrecking ball fist the gold rained out of the pot like sparkling glass
Like a flash of lightning I zoomed over and filled my pockets with glory
Till they were stuffed like Christmas turkeys
The ogre carried me home like a king on a horse.

Roman Elliss (7)
Nottingham High Infant & Junior School, Nottingham

Last Minute Winner

It was the final five minutes of the game
The crowd were on the edge of their seats
The score was tied like a tightrope
Fans shouting, clapping and chanting like in a One Direction concert

The dancing football was coloured in strawberry laces and orange gummy bears as it boomed forward
My shiny back boots sparkled on the lush green grass
I felt the pain in my legs as they started to ache
Suddenly the ball was at my feet, but stood in front were two angry defenders
I ran as fast as a cheetah so I could go past them

To my surprise, I was standing in front of the goal
The crowd roared with excitement
I took aim and charged my legs
Bang!
The ball flew like an acrobat dodging the goalkeeper's hand
I jumped with joy as I knew I scored the winning goal.

Zain Khan (10)
Nottingham High Infant & Junior School, Nottingham

Dreamland

Whoosh
We are now in Dreamland
Where anything can happen
Jake is as brave as an ox
As sly as a fox
He will be our hero today
Scared, he wakes up
A shiver runs down his spine
Today is the day
He will face demons and devils
With his bare hands
Swords clash together
Like a head-on collision
Scared, you keep on fighting
Hurt, you have to carry on
Sad things will happen
This will be a hard task
The devils have no fear
This is Skyland
Small islands float in the air
It is a beautiful place
But at 6am
You wake up to find it's a dream
Anything can happen in dreams

It's exciting
It feels amazing
When can I go back?
I still need to defeat the evil devil
And get the old breath-taking castle back.

Gabe Edwards (11)
Nottingham High Infant & Junior School, Nottingham

Once Upon A Dream

I dreamed a dream in bed last night
Of places most bizarre
Of enormous chocolate shopping malls
And lots of ugly bridge trolls

Of bubbly Fanta waterfalls
And loud echoing calls
And wizards casting magic spells
Using lots of brain cells

Of huge marshmallow trampolines
And wow, amazing Haribo machines
Now just look at the sky and wait
You'll see my Mars bar, mate!

And oh how many things I saw
But no, there's still more and more
Now my feet are getting lousy
But now hour by hour I'm getting more drowsy

Now I'm falling asleep
And I'm looking like a creep
Oh no, my hairs are getting curled
And I need to exit this world!

Saketh Chinta (8)
Nottingham High Infant & Junior School, Nottingham

Fly, Fly, Fly!

Sleeping
I had a big, colossal dream
What would it be like to fly?
Imagine that!
As you whoosh through the air like a fighter jet
And you score the winning goal
Driving flying cars to many planets and moons
And relax in your flying house

Everything becomes futuristic
Everything is operated by voice command
Go through rapid flying time machines
And live in the year 10982589!
I woke up...
Something weird happened to my house

I looked through my diamond windows
I realised my dream came true!
My house was mysteriously flying and everything was operated by voice command!
I once had a big, massive dream
It will always remain great as it changed my whole life!

Shuban Yadavakrishnan (9)
Nottingham High Infant & Junior School, Nottingham

Once Upon A Dream

I dreamed a dream in bed last night
Of places most bizarre
I jumped in the deep water
And saw a great white shark
His name was Jaws
He was a killing machine
A deadly creature too

But if I found another one
The others would be chasing me
I needed to hide, I needed to run
But where would I run?
I didn't know
But somewhere!

Where was a spot?
There was one
A little crack
I got in it
Would he see me?

I had a plan
Try to lose him
Good plan
I lost him, yes
There in the crack

There I was safe
Oh no, there he was
He could get in the crack
Oh no, he ate me!

Benjamin Chadwick (8)
Nottingham High Infant & Junior School, Nottingham

I Have A Pokémon Dream

I have a dream of being a Pokémon
Whether it's a flying type
A grass type
Or a fire type
I have a dream of being a
Pokémon

I will fight against other Pokémon at my own will
I will be the legendary Latios and soar through the sky
I will be the legendary Kyogre and swim through the Hoenn Sea
Or I will be a normal Wurmple and wander in the grass

Whatever Pokémon I am
I don't care
As long as I am a Pokémon

I will be
As fierce as a dinosaur
As courageous as a mountaineer
And as cool as Catwoman's cat!

But the truth is
That I am Rayquaza.

Yusuf Butt (9)
Nottingham High Infant & Junior School, Nottingham

Wake Up

London is black in this world...
Skies are grey and buildings smashed
Bats and crows rest on the shattered face of Big Ben
Whilst Buckingham Palace lies still, not a soul alive
Sinister black double-decker buses drive endlessly
And unmanned grey taxi cabs; silent, waiting...
I appear at King's Cross next
Beside me are lifeless trains, dark and ominous
The tormenting moon shines through the station
Teasing and taunting
Creak!
And the floor begins to rattle...
The lights of the haunting trains turn on as if they are watching me
I jump back in fear
The moon cackles and shines its blinding light near
I fall...
And wake up.

Ishan Feroz (10)
Nottingham High Infant & Junior School, Nottingham

One Day Everything Changed

One day everything changed all of a sudden
But it was amazing, the trees smelt like lollipops
And water tasted like Coke

Then I met this folk who is now
My best friend
I do not know how
It all happened
All of a sudden
I thought this could be my dream land
One hour later I met Ronaldo
Messi, Ibrahimovic, Pogba and Neymar
After, we did everything fun
Things that I never did before
Everything changed there
There were no homeless people
Because I grew
Bread, fruits and everything else for them
The best bit is that
I went to my public swimming pool
And it was full of sweets and chocolate
What a dream.

Jagpal Singh (10)
Nottingham High Infant & Junior School, Nottingham

Sports Car Dream

In a dream I had last night
Long after I turned out the light
I heard a noise long and loud
Around my dream it did resound
My bed started to change shape
And when I looked I had to gape
The bed legs were now wheels
Being held back by brakes that squealed!
The duvet flung above my head
Made the bonnet and roof crimson red
My mattress formed into heated seats
Leather replaced my soft bed sheets
The pillow now felt like rocks
Because it had become the engine box
As I zoomed around people watched in awe
Because my bed made a resounding roar!
After I zoomed around a racetrack
I awoke and wished I could get that dream back.

Ben French (9)
Nottingham High Infant & Junior School, Nottingham

I Have A Dream Poem

If I could dream any dream it would be
A samurai sword battle
On the mountains of Japan
The snow as white
As a cloud on a hot summer's day
The battle would be held at the famous temple of light
Under the moon with a cheesy grin
The swords would be as long as an elephant's trunk
A bell would ring as loud as a phone
Both of the fighters would jump into battle
Swords in front, hoping to kill
Clash went the swords all day long
For three long days no one would've won
Until both of them die of dehydration
Yes this may be a lesson to you
But whenever you go into battle
Always bring some water.

Alec Sehat (9)
Nottingham High Infant & Junior School, Nottingham

Another Day Of Defence

It all began at ten in the morning
I heard a noise as loud as an exploding strawberry
Which meant it was time for zombies to be decapitated
Which leads to another day of defence

Rushing downstairs I see a giant robot with two lamp posts as his arms
Then I realise this will be no problem
Especially with my apple-core throwing plant

A few minutes later I realise the land on the left is getting overrun
So I rush back in the house to get the coconut cannon
I tell him to use his power-up which he does
And *kabam!* All zombies have been decapitated

And that was my fifteenth day on defence.

Toyan Garland (10)
Nottingham High Infant & Junior School, Nottingham

Once Upon A Dream

I dreamed in bed last night
Of places most bizarre
I had a fight
With a pixie armed with a jar

The whole story
I'll tell you now
Although it is gory
Still makes me feel like a silly cow

Tinker Bell strolled up to me
With venom in her eyes
Holding something that shone brightly
Hurled it at me like custard cream pies

One thousand pixies were behind her
I made a mistake
And called them vulgar
Someone threw a cake

Whoosh! The cake flew through the air
Boom! It hit my head
Icing stuck to my hair
Suddenly I woke up in bed.

Esme Winter (9)
Nottingham High Infant & Junior School, Nottingham

Numana

Everything was quiet like a desert
Just that there was a green land
There, where he stood
Crunch! went the grass
Which danced with the light breeze
As he tiptoed through the land

Soon the coast arrived
The glistening sand
Which ran away as the sea came back
There he stood silent like an owl
The ocean with the tiny sand granules
Felt like a smooth carpet
Where right next to it
Lay a cliffside as rugged as a shell

He bent over and touched the sand
It felt so smooth
The sea had an emerald colour
He wondered if he would ever find a place
As magic as this again.

Jack Battisti Downey (10)
Nottingham High Infant & Junior School, Nottingham

Under The Misty Mountains

Under the misty mountains the dragon roars in rage
It was the noble traveller coming for his riches
The spires loomed over them like the summer sun
Running up the stairs, well it all began to shake

Regretting the choice they made
The cave began to get so hot
The burning fire brought down it all
It was the dragon of the cave, it came down to kill them all

The rocks began to crack and scream
The gold began to bubble and squeak
It was the burning fire breaking up the walls

Still as a statue the mountains were
The gold seeped through the cracks in the rocks, making a golden mountain.

Robert James Henry Goodwin (11)
Nottingham High Infant & Junior School, Nottingham

I Wish I Could Remember My Dreams

I wish I could remember my dreams
They disappear, like pupils at the end of the school day
I sometimes think I've got it, but then no
Like a sandcastle on a beach, it washes away

But sometimes I am happy that I can't remember my dreams
Relive the time you got chased by a bear
Or fell off a balancing beam
Why would anyone want to be reminded of a nightmare?

Maybe someone will invent a machine to help me remember my dreams
But I only want to know if it's joyful or exciting
I don't want to worry about what my dreams mean
They should remain a mystery, a secret, never to be seen.

William Oliver James Harwood (9)
Nottingham High Infant & Junior School, Nottingham

I Have A Dream

I have a dream that there is no school
I can stay at home all day
Play, play and only play
I can do all sorts of different activities
Like play cricket outdoors
Or badminton indoors
I can play electronic or board games
I can go for a long walk

I have a dream
I could bake every day
And eat cake every day
I don't have to brush every day
Like dinosaurs who don't brush any day
I wish
Dinosaurs were still alive
They are nice, calm and friendly
My favourite one is a velociraptor called Clive
Because he is very clumsy
I still wish that I could run as fast as Clive!

Namit Batra (9)
Nottingham High Infant & Junior School, Nottingham

Siberian Nightmare

Fear shook his brain
His mind began filling with thoughts
With dark thoughts
Of pain, tyranny and death

These cold nights were the worst
The wind was raging
Shadows roamed these dreams
Shadows that went unseen

The blood-red walls were lined with chains
Restricting the movement of the unlucky few
Those unlucky few battered and bruised
Their faces the victims of battery and torture

Siberia was the past
Yet for him it is the present
The Cold War is over
But not for him

He escaped the torture
But only if he could escape it in his dreams.

Harry Goonan (9)
Nottingham High Infant & Junior School, Nottingham

The Ride

I sit in the car
The metal bar descends
I am cold and scared
But excited

Look ahead, we start to move
A drop is ahead, steep, long
Goosebumps dimple my arms

Clattering, clanking we climb
Getting faster and faster but still
We are a snail

My tummy goes all tingly
Just as I reach the dive
The sky rushes away and
The ground rushes up

My face goes like ice
And the trees blur
The crowds of people look like clothes
Abruptly we come to a halt
The metal bars are raised
We step dizzy out of the dream land

Again!

Nathan Chadwick (11)
Nottingham High Infant & Junior School, Nottingham

The Magical Forest

Once upon a dream, two explorers as brave as lions,
Went to a snake-infested forest.

'Shall we go yet?' said one.
'Let's pack,' said the other.

Off they went, into the dark, slimy forest,
With bags as fat as rhinoceroses.

The ground seemed to slither and hiss,
Long, green snakes appeared, under every tree in sight.

'Eek!' the explorers screamed,
As loud as a monkey dropping its banana!

Back they ran,
Back to their soft, comfy beds,
Back to sleep.
Zzzz
To dream the exact same dream...

James Golding (7)
Nottingham High Infant & Junior School, Nottingham

Once Upon A Dream

A bee was buzzing around a flower
like a lawnmower
I was made up of ice cream,
Once upon a dream
I popped the bubbles with my fingers,
whilst eating fish fingers
The bus was as big as a tortoise's shell
and it looked like it was time for the school bell
My school was built with jelly, topped with cream
Once upon a dream!!
Once upon a dream!!

The rocket zoomed to Planet Earth
heading towards north,
Clouds were as fluffy as candyfloss
just like a shiny gloss
I then woke up with a scream,
Once upon a dream!!
Once upon a dream!!

Om Kamath (7)
Nottingham High Infant & Junior School, Nottingham

Once Upon A Dream

I dreamed a dream in bed last night
Of places most bizarre
Of vampires and witches who always have itches
And werewolves who were scared of fleas
Of mummies and zombies that were scared of candy
Well who really cares about that?
All of a sudden a cat burst into my poem
But actually that cat was scared of a bat
The bat was scared of a hat
But the hat was scared of a bat
There once was a ghoul
He thought he was so cool
But he wasn't a cool ghoul, because he was so ugly
He looked in a mirror and it cracked
All of a sudden I woke up
And the demons were surrounding me.

Matthew Moran (8)
Nottingham High Infant & Junior School, Nottingham

The Big Chocolate House

Drip... drip... drip
Went the massive, tasty chocolate all night
Solid chocolatey walls that won't fall
That are made with gooey toffee popcorn
Chunky chimneys releasing chocolatey smoke on the rooftops
Chocolatey bunnies laughing and jumping
Up and down in the living room
Whoosh! went the chocolate river
The chocolate AC cooling everyone down
I sit on the chocolate muffin watching 'Charlie and the Chocolate Factory'
Free chocolate money as much as you want
This house is a popular landmark where
People gather to enjoy healthy chocolate milkshakes.

Aarush Anand (7)
Nottingham High Infant & Junior School, Nottingham

Dreaming A Dream

I dreamed a dream in bed last night
Of places most bizarre
Of candy lands and witches' feet
And hamsters that played guitar
I dreamed of cows in space
And chickens that played the bass
I dreamed of oxes in boxes
Such a weird and wonderful place
I dreamed of car chases and pigs doing up laces
Such a magical and mysterious world
I dreamed of cats chasing purple rats
Such a funny and fast-paced dream
I dreamed of funny faces and babies taking paces
I went through time drinking lovely wine
But now morning is dawning
And my dream is but a distant glow.

Henry Strudwick (8)
Nottingham High Infant & Junior School, Nottingham

Once Upon A Dream

When I close my eyes at night
I think about such things
Of chocolate cake and
Dogs called Cocoa living in my house

Sometimes I dream of other things
Of monkeys in the trees
I swing with them from branch to branch
Until it's time to rest

Sometimes my dreams are not so fun
With English all day long
With not a break in sight
But then I wake and breathe a sigh
Relief is what I feel!

I like to dream and travel far
On the currents of my mind
They take me where I like to go
To places out of this world.

Isak Ibrahim (11)
Nottingham High Infant & Junior School, Nottingham

My Dream

I dreamed a dream last night
Of spiders and apples attacking me
Ducks playing the drums, sweets and marshmallows raining down
And the sun changing colour every second

Houses changing shape, water slides for stairs
Killing clowns attacking everyone
And rulers dancing everywhere
Grass flying up to space and changing colour

I dreamed a dream last night
Of spiders and apples attacking me
Ducks playing the drums, sweets and marshmallows raining down
The sun changing colour every second
Houses changing shape, water slides for stairs.

Aditya Puri (8)
Nottingham High Infant & Junior School, Nottingham

The Dream

I dreamed a dream in bed last night
Of cotton candy walls
And wafer screens everywhere
And flying chocolate frogs

Of butterbeer as rain
And melted caramel rivers
Of sweet vans for transportation
And Coca-Cola as medicine

What paradise it is
And upside-down Pikachus
Drinking chocolate rivers
And almighty cheeseburgers

Candy skyscrapers
That reach into space
And diamond clocks
That tick like mad

But bye-bye
I'd like to go
Because the almighty
Illuminati are coming!

Thales Iliadis (10)
Nottingham High Infant & Junior School, Nottingham

My Magical Underwater Dream

Slowly I drift off to my magical underwater world
It is peaceful, calm and light rays look curled
I can breathe underwater in my dream
I am happy, no need to panic, shout or scream
My dolphin friend comes to greet me
I hold on tightly to his fin
And as we zoom along I feel so free
My body is weightless, there is no sound
I have so much confidence, I know I won't be drowned
We are on an adventure to seek precious sea crystals
Hidden in caves where the sea is shallow and ripples
But beware of the ferocious sea dragons
That guard the gems.

Max Morgan (7)
Nottingham High Infant & Junior School, Nottingham

Dull Vs Imagination

I lived in a dull house made out of dirt
It smelled like rotten egg and it was as boring as walking
One day I walked down the grey street, then *bang!*
A magic gate appeared made out of rainbow
That seemed to smile at me
I went back home and got my bony dog
I went through the gate like a raging bull
I found a mythical telescope
That allowed me to look at people's dreams
I saw trolls and candyfloss clouds
I heard bangs, booms and fizzes
I decided to make my house here
I had a good time and never went back to the dull place again.

Jack Aram (7)
Nottingham High Infant & Junior School, Nottingham

A World Of Twisted Colours

In a world just like ours
Where only the colours are back to front
Like a cart pulling a horse
Or even Jerry and Tom
It can often be a bit costly
To have the lights on all night
To keep it dark

I'm slowly getting used to this topsy-turvy world
Where bushes are as red as postboxes should be
And strawberries are as green as grass
I finally realised that green means stop
And red means go
Which explains why people were beeping at me
At the traffic lights
And now I understand why the sky is blue
Like a banana.

Leon Elliss (10)
Nottingham High Infant & Junior School, Nottingham

Giant Zombie Bees!

You might think, what are Zombie Bees?
They are as bouncy as a tennis ball
As big as footballs
And as hard as robots
Their sting is as poisonous as snake venom
And their fur is as green as grass
And they are as scary as trolls

At first they came through my windows
And tried to attack me
So I got out my Los Angeles Dodgers baseball bat
And started to hit them with it
One went and pinged out the window
And all of them started flying away
Everything went blurry
I suddenly woke up to realise
It was all a dream.

Ethan Pickering (9)
Nottingham High Infant & Junior School, Nottingham

Snow Fun

Flying through the night sky with clouds whooshing by
In the aeroplane
I see stars sparkling like diamonds
The aeroplane glides then becomes slower and slower
The bus takes us to a mountain up a road
That snakes left and right
The snow is as white as clouds
The button lift pulls like I'm riding an elastic band
The snow is sleeping on the ground
Then I fall on the ground with a bang
It is as fun as going down a water slide
I go down the hill with the cold wind in my face
And look forward to the hot chocolate that warms my tummy.

Georgia Grace Aram (7)
Nottingham High Infant & Junior School, Nottingham

The Castle

One day I was walking my horse
His name was Joe
Then I saw a castle made of chocolate with caramel roof tiles
With a chocolate fountain and a hard toffee door
With a candy cane rock spire
Then I went into the castle, then I saw the king
He was eating toffee apples and cakes
He was as greedy as a pig
Then I slept on a bit of wood
'Argh!' I screamed
Then all the soldiers put me in a prison
It was as small as a suitcase
Then I saw a hole
I climbed into the hole and *splash!*
I fell into the sewer side.

Eron Singh Dhami (7)
Nottingham High Infant & Junior School, Nottingham

Arsenal 1-0 Tottenham

The sun glared over the pitch.
Was it a dream?
Alexis Sanchez asked me to
Play on his team.

He passed me the ball
And I kicked a real cracker.
It flew through the air
Straight to Granit Xhaka.

He passed it to me
And I knew what to do.
I did my best and
into the net the ball flew.

I put my arms out wide
In a dream-like state
And the crowd roared, 'Ruben!
You are great!'

The sun set high
At Highbury Hill
Arsenal - one
Tottenham - nil.

Ruben Evans (8)
Nottingham High Infant & Junior School, Nottingham

Untitled

I dreamed a dream in bed last night
Of melted chocolate in my mouth
Of marshmallow cars on a football pitch
And a candy army outside

Of driving in a limousine
And living in a candy tree
With chocolate monkeys dancing
And being cheered by my fans

Of being the king of the world
And clowns breaking their legs
With a bathtub full of caramel
And dancing with some chickens

Of pigs wearing wigs
And flying with a jetpack
With a giant cake with sprinkles on
And cow mouths on fire!

Taran Sabarinathan (8)
Nottingham High Infant & Junior School, Nottingham

The Space Crocodile

One day in my home
A space crocodile came
He was as blue as the sky
On a hot summer's day
He was in a pirate hat
And the rest of the gear too
Then he said, 'I will kill your dad
And eat him for my tea too!'
Then he covered my mouth with Sellotape
And I felt scared like a beetle about to be squashed
Then the crocodile walked like a penguin
Into the pit trap
I set it because I knew he was coming
Because I had a dream
And I saw his green slimy alien blood
And it made me scream
'Eeeek!'

Maxwell Cooper (7)
Nottingham High Infant & Junior School, Nottingham

The Dream

I dreamed a dream in bed last night
Of melted chocolate baths
And chickens dancing in the streets
With massively long paths

Of people flying over me
And guns shooting loudly
Of massive people crying
And everyone sleeping soundly

Of cats wearing hats of money
With people dabbing everywhere
Of people throwing pies
But no one actually cares

Of cats eating hot dogs
And elephants squashing pigs
Of gingerbread men roaming streets
Such things like people wearing wigs.

Samuel Grayton (8)
Nottingham High Infant & Junior School, Nottingham

Flying Through The Sky

I'm flying, I'm flying, meandering through the sky
Oh what a beautiful sight, it's like going through a clot of candyfloss

Trees are as small as ants and houses are like crumbs
The hills were the sandy dunes of the desert

I'm going at lightning speed, whooshing like a rocket
I'm a shooting star zooming through the sky

The sun is as hot as fire and I was levitating in its direction
My body was exhausted like a sloth

I woke up and realised it was a delightful dream.

Lohit Deepak (10)
Nottingham High Infant & Junior School, Nottingham

Once Upon A Dream

I dreamed a dream in bed last night
Of places most bizarre
I took Virgin Galactic to space
And looked at all the stars

I went to Jupiter and saw Saturn
And, wow, it was so far
I saw a star shining bright
In fact it was the brightest star

I went on lots of space walks
And I could float about
It was really, really, really fun
And that's without a doubt

Then I went back home to Earth
But as I was getting out
I was sure I saw an alien
Wandering about!

Nathan Sood-Patel (8)
Nottingham High Infant & Junior School, Nottingham

Planet Chaos

I step outside my front door into a completely different world and gasp
The sky is as green as a pea, the ground is as blue as the sea
Trees sprout from candyfloss clouds
Houses lay on their backs wowed
Dogs fly around my head, howling to be fed
There is no time, no forecast can predict the random clime
The BFG is changed to the BEG
His eyes glow red, his evil laugh shakes his head
The Iron Man soars through the air like an aeroplane booming, 'Stop!'
My alarm clock beep, beep, beeps, *whoop!*

Kitty Strudwick (7)
Nottingham High Infant & Junior School, Nottingham

The Gladiator Boy

I am in a dark and gloomy hotel room
The phone rings, loudly I answer, it is Dr Doom!
'I've got your powerless president
Meet me in an hour.'
He is locked and trapped in steel chains at the top of Freedom Tower
I felt determined and dashed to my car as quick as lightning
I was excited but still frightened
However, I had to be brave, I had a president to save
I sped over the Hudson River
The skyscrapers as tall as a giant
Peered over the city colourful and vibrant.

Ben Massey (8)
Nottingham High Infant & Junior School, Nottingham

Midnight Dragon

In my dream in the night
I saw a dragon in the light
I really did get a fright
I wondered if it was going to bite!
It stared at me with beady eyes
Then it whimpered and began to cry
I was so sad, I felt quite bad
I really got mad with my iPad
It didn't work, I could not see
Why this machine was bothering me
'Can you help me?'
'Yes,' I said, 'I can.'
Then the dragon and I were best friends
We sat and played till the dream did end.

Jacob Thomas (8)
Nottingham High Infant & Junior School, Nottingham

I Dreamed A Dream...

I dreamed a dream in bed last night
Of Moonface dancing on a pie
Chickens playing the guitar
A guy fighting a bath

Winning one billion pounds
Being the best cricketer in the world
Hearing funny sounds
Diving into a chocolate bath

Becoming an undercover spy
Saucepan Man playing the guitar
Of being a famous footballer
Cats holding hot dogs

Mrs Bailey dabbing
Roald Dahl still alive
Making massive padding
My own baby bear.

Joshua Parsons (8)
Nottingham High Infant & Junior School, Nottingham

The Dream

I dreamed a dream in bed last night
Of meatballs blowing up
Talking burgers
Dancing chickens nearly made me wake up

Footballs flying everywhere
Singing kittens
Monkeys making dinner
People upside down

Trees made of carrots
Alarms going off everywhere
Tomatoes riding motorbikes
Spaghetti soaring through the sky
Of sweetcorn eating pie

Dancing hot dogs
Marshmallows walking on the street
Giraffes touching their feet.

Sasmeet Satyam (8)
Nottingham High Infant & Junior School, Nottingham

Once Upon A Dream

I dreamed a dream in bed last night
I was riding on a whale gliding through the stars
The night was black
The whale was flying low, I could see some fancy cars

The battle below was big
There was cattle wearing wigs
There were crabs in a bath mixed with fish
People were eating pigs

The whale was big and blue
With a tail as big as a double decker bus
I have to admit that it was desperate for the loo
There were lots of bats making a big fuss.

James Freeston (8)
Nottingham High Infant & Junior School, Nottingham

I Had A Dream

Once I had a dream where
I lived in a candy house
With a
Bubblegum trampoline
Firing me into cotton candy clouds

Through colourful sticky toffee windows
I could see chocolate ducks
On a lemonade lake

A spiral fruit winder chimney
Over a roaring Haribo fire
With a gummy cat
On a gummy mat

A gigantic liquorice wood
And a fragrant lollipop garden

Once I had a dream
And this was mine.

Harry Elwick (9)
Nottingham High Infant & Junior School, Nottingham

The Dream

I dreamed a dream in bed last night
Of humans burping buses
And dancing babies with shades

I dreamed a dream in bed last night
Of places most bizarre
Of flying hippos running down
And enslaved ants dancing like an Egyptian

Of baboons driving lorries
Of farting chickens
And cats driving rockets

I dreamed an amazing dream
Of nightmares dying
Of Lego dragons driven by me
And I woke with a rainbow chicken on me!

Sam Grady (8)
Nottingham High Infant & Junior School, Nottingham

Dream Land

I dreamed a dream in bed last night
Of places so funny
Of marshmallows raining down
Of houses made of candy

And lakes of melted chocolate
Of baboons driving gigantic cars
And dragons flying upside down
Monkeys dancing in outer space

Of turkeys driving tuk tuks
Of people going *cluck, cluck*
Of watermelons surfing
And humans hanging from trees

Of meatballs wearing diving suits
And flying megalodons!

Ayotunde Adewoye (8)
Nottingham High Infant & Junior School, Nottingham

The Day I Saw A Martian

I saw a space station in the sky
With flying saucers whizzing by,
Martians with laser guns
Eating squishy, yellow buns.

What are cities like on Mars?
Skyscrapers that reach the stars,
Shops selling red Smartie pops,
Martians wait at spaceship stops.

I would like to meet these guys
Although they do come from the skies.
'Greetings Martian,' I would say,
'You really should come here to stay'.

James Bowden (9)
Nottingham High Infant & Junior School, Nottingham

I Have A Dream

I have a dream that every person should play cricket
Because it's exciting when the ball hits the wicket!
'Howzat!' your fellow players scream
You're on the way to being the winning team!
The lawns are grassy, glossy and green
It's the best type of surface I've ever seen!
The wicket keeper is as agile as a cat
Personally, I like to bat
I wish my dream would come true
You may disagree
But play it and see.

Kapil Krishanand (9)
Nottingham High Infant & Junior School, Nottingham

A Good, Good Dream

I had a dream, it was so good
There was a ladybird sitting on my rug
It looked like a cherry on a little beach

I had a dream, it was so good
There was a farmer drinking from my cup
He was quite pale, believe me!

I had a dream, it was so good
There was a boy sitting on a tree
He was like a chimpanzee

I had a dream, it was so good
There was me writing this poem on
Thursday 13th October!

Oscar Armson (7)
Nottingham High Infant & Junior School, Nottingham

Fast Cars

I had a fast car that was fast as lightning
It was so fast you couldn't see it.
I had a fast car that was fast as a cheetah

I had a fast car that was faster than a Porsche.
I had a fast car, which was fast as a bullet
I had a fast car, more powerful than a rocket
I had a fast car that became invisible
I had a fast car that travelled into the future.
I once had a car that became my friend.
I miss you my car.

Nico Bains (7)
Nottingham High Infant & Junior School, Nottingham

My Granny Had A Ferrari

I dreamed a dream in bed last night
Of giants playing football
Of chips flying everywhere
And school will only let us play

I dreamed a dream in bed last night
Of me being the best football player in the world
Of Arun being nicer
And my granny having a Ferrari

I dreamed a dream in bed last night
Of Mrs Bailey doing a mini dab
Of monkeys playing chess
And dogs playing American football.

Mandip Singh Leihal (10)
Nottingham High Infant & Junior School, Nottingham

Once Upon A Dream

I dreamed a dream in bed last night
Of places most bizarre
I was stuck in marshmallows
Eating them all up on my own

Soon only some marshmallows are left
So I let them be
Instead of eating I thought
What else could I do?
So I jumped up and down on my own

I jumped back down into Earth
And landed in my chimney
Hearing my TV running
And my parents eating so much pudding.

George Thompson (9)
Nottingham High Infant & Junior School, Nottingham

I Had A Dream

I once had a dream
A very funny dream
Where pigs went *quack* and the lazy cows went *oink!*
A place where clever instruments played themselves
And everything was made of sweet cookie dough
Where cars were as fast as a bullet
One of the shops was called Big Bouncy Balloons
But before I could do anything
I heard a voice saying, 'Wake up!'
I hope I can get back to this dream tomorrow night.

Taylor Bradley (10)
Nottingham High Infant & Junior School, Nottingham

Once Upon A Dream

I dreamed a dream in bed last night
Of places most bizarre
Of candy houses, chocolate ponds
With people drinking hard

Jelly bean cellos and such fun
With the fiddle a whole band to listen

A crisp-made airport
With a Coke-made plane
Such burps on the flight
With an M&M sight

A land of delights with such good light
In the sight
With movies at night.

Euan Dodd (8)
Nottingham High Infant & Junior School, Nottingham

Untitled

I dreamed a dream, in bed, last night
Of places most bizarre
Of candy-coated doors and musical floors
A giant ox and a huge boombox
In the middle of the land, playing lots of famous bands
But then the power cut down
And the ox started to frown
The land appeared to turn brown
Then I saw a king with a crown
He said, 'Wake up, you're covered in muck!'
Then I said, 'Just my luck!'

George Akins (8)
Nottingham High Infant & Junior School, Nottingham

The Dream

I dreamed a dream in bed last night
Of marshmallows playing the guitar
Dancing dinosaurs, it was so bizarre
And giants the size of newborn babies

Baboons wearing orange peels
And babies going to the moon
Popstar seals driving a bus
Builders using spoons to build

Monkeys swimming in the sea
Seals in a circus
Burgers dancing at the canteen
And driving a private plane.

Nathan Samuel (8)
Nottingham High Infant & Junior School, Nottingham

A Terrifying Night

All I see is darkness all around me
I'm alone in a dark jungle
I hear bats screeching and ghosts whispering
I feel a rat's tail whipping against my leg
I'm petrified and trembling with fear
Never will I get out of here
I feel my feet sinking into a swamp
I grab what I think is a vine
I'm swinging across crocodiles' spiky backs
I'm petrified and trembling with fear!

Umair Hurairah Nazir (7)
Nottingham High Infant & Junior School, Nottingham

Flight

I dreamt that I could fly
And travel through the air
I lived in a house made of cloud
With toffee tables and chairs

I had a staircase made of jelly
With chocolate covered walls
My sink poured out biscuits
And cotton candy balls

I would stay in my house all day
And travel through the night
I'm like an aeroplane
When it's taking flight.

Ryan Mannion (9)
Nottingham High Infant & Junior School, Nottingham

Vegetable Oceans

I dreamed a dream in bed last night
Of places most bizarre
Of dancing carrots and big, strange fish
Playing with a purple jar

There were green and orange jellyfish
And I saw a whale shark
Yellow peppers and orange too
I saw an ocean park

I saw a jiving cucumber
I saw a giant peach
I saw a jolly octopus
Singing, 'I love a sandy beach!'

Anna Ratan (8)
Nottingham High Infant & Junior School, Nottingham

The Dream

I dreamed a dream in bed last night
Of my sister turning into ice cream
Of blueberries fighting bananas
And the world turning into whipped cream

Of the Colosseum turning into a doughnut
Of rocks turning into cake
And my dad is David Beckham

Of the moon turning into cheese
Of the undead coming to life
And the illuminati doing the dab!

James Black (10)
Nottingham High Infant & Junior School, Nottingham

The Flying Rock

I dream of dreams
My dreams are funny
My dreams are weird
One day I dreamed of a flying rock
All I saw was a red shining rock
Flying high, up in the sky
Up went the flying rock
To the stars and to reach the sun
The sun was like a ball of fire
We jumped into the ball of fire
Played a lot with melting lava
Back on the flying rock, off I went home.

Rishi Gouni (7)
Nottingham High Infant & Junior School, Nottingham

Once Upon A Football Dream

Lionel Messi gave me a call
To ask if I wanted to play football.
He said he was one man down,
So I rushed into Barcelona town
Neymar said I saved the day,
When I arrived at Camp Nou to play.
I helped them score the winning goal -
I dug them out of a great big hole!
The World Cup jumped into my hands
The crowd were cheering in the stands!!

Edward Mellors (7)
Nottingham High Infant & Junior School, Nottingham

Once Upon A Dream

I dreamed a dream in bed last night
Of places most bizarre
Of Justin Bieber playing duck guitars
And Michael Jackson playing jelly cellos
Justin Bieber performed a backflip and landed on a house
But Michael Jackson rode on a dog like a professional
Then Justin Bieber got out a microphone and sang
Jelly beans were on grass ducks in rivers.

Marley Parejo (8)
Nottingham High Infant & Junior School, Nottingham

The Night Star

Once I had a dream
I saw a shining star
Running across the sky
First I was on the grass
Then suddenly I went into another dimension
I found myself in a world full of brightness and nature
It was confusing my brain
I walked up to a tree with something on it
It was a bright white star
Suddenly I fell into a dark hole
Then I woke up.

Alfie Armstrong (7)
Nottingham High Infant & Junior School, Nottingham

My Sleeping Pirate Ship

I drift to sleep in a bed as soft as a cloud,
I begin to dream, a dream that starts off loud!
I'm in a pirate ship in the middle of a ferocious storm,
A wave splashes upon me and my crew, the water is the opposite of warm.

We're under attack!
But I need a snack...
What to do?
Save my crew?
Or have a Jammy Dodger or two??

Ollie Hustwayte (9)
Nottingham High Infant & Junior School, Nottingham

Sweet Sweet Land

Sweet Land is a magical place
Full of every imaginable taste
There are candyfloss clouds and loads of candy rain
Haribo bears walking upstairs
And houses made of chocolate pears
There are toffee seats that you really could eat
Marshmallow beds to rest your heads
Do you want to come to Sweet Land?
Come with me, I will take your hand.

Oscar G C Gisborne (7)
Nottingham High Infant & Junior School, Nottingham

Once Upon A Dream

A place for the homeless, the taps pour out Coke and Fanta
A river made out of Fanta, Coke and best of all, water
Trees fall to the ground like a pot of water upside down

A light that shines brighter
Than a sword made out of fire
All of the cushions feel like a bear's fur
I woke up, that was a good dream.

Nihal Singh (7)
Nottingham High Infant & Junior School, Nottingham

Mine Base

I dream I am on a raft
In the world of Minecraft
I am in a dark, deep cave and my family is brave
And then there is a zombie attack!
But I hit back
Off goes Mr Zombie in the lava
And that's the end of this palaver
Emeralds, diamonds, friends and family
Now we all are living happily.

Farris Hameed (7)
Nottingham High Infant & Junior School, Nottingham

Once Upon A Dream

I dreamed a dream in bed last night
Of places most bizarre
I was in a haunted house and a strange ghost played a guitar
He had a cowboy hat on
And a black cat on a mat

My friend, Matthew, stroked the cat
But the cat smacked Matthew's leg
He squealed and said, 'Argh!'

Alfie Cooper (8)
Nottingham High Infant & Junior School, Nottingham

Once Upon A Dream

I dreamed a dream in bed last night
Of places most bizarre
Of green sharks with arms
And fish that play guitars
And of pigs that are clean

Of fish that have legs which are also red
And red cats which chase purple rats
And blue kangaroos
Chasing orange cockapoos.

Josiah Ibrahim (9)
Nottingham High Infant & Junior School, Nottingham

Untitled

I dreamed a dream in bed last night
Of humans visiting outer space
Of ghosts invading the world
And ending up in Pirate World

I dreamed a dream in bed last night
Of cats wearing banana peels
Of spacemen falling down to Earth
And me ending up in a gingerbread house.

Ethan Corne (8)
Nottingham High Infant & Junior School, Nottingham

Dragon Dream

Up in the sky, past the birds
The roar of dragons can be heard
The icy-cold or red-hot lava
The earthy-green who is my father

The Electrots hang around bold
As fast as lightning we are told
The icy-cold will fall and fail
The crazy lava as slow as a snail.

Oliver James Hetfield (11)
Nottingham High Infant & Junior School, Nottingham

Once Upon A Dream

I dreamed a dream in bed last night
Of places most bizarre
Of candy lands and chocolate plans
And with a caramel car

With parallel lines of mints everywhere
There were pines and
Marshmallows going round and round
I fell on the ground and flew inbound.

Fletcher Phoenix (8)
Nottingham High Infant & Junior School, Nottingham

Dreams

D reams are weird and wonderful
R epeated they may be, but some are fearful like a nightmare
E xciting like fire or dull like a lesson
A mazing or weird like a two-headed donkey
M anky like cheese or complicated like maths, now that's a dream.

George Emerson (9)
Nottingham High Infant & Junior School, Nottingham

Once Upon A Dream

My bed's a boat sailing out to sea
Passing many islands full of fantasy
Promising excitement and mystery
Each night a different destination
I wonder where my boat will take me
Tonight I hope it's about pirates raiding
A treasure island many miles away.

Alfie Armson (9)
Nottingham High Infant & Junior School, Nottingham

I Dreamed A Dream

I dreamed a dream in bed last night
Of crazy candy trees;
Of magical chocolate springs and lakes
And amazing candy bees

Of giant marshmallow monsters
And clouds of whipped cream.
Of massive tasty treacle waves
And misty yellow streams.

George William Turton (8)
Nottingham High Infant & Junior School, Nottingham

The Dream

I dreamed a dream in bed last night
Of marshmallow clouds so warm and soft
Of rivers and lakes of Slush Puppie
And an atmosphere of candyfloss

Of marshmallow and Smartie toadstools
Of sherbet grass
Of Flake trees
And shoe lace leaves.

Michael James Syme-Grant (10)
Nottingham High Infant & Junior School, Nottingham

Candy Land

Candy Land as pretty as rainbows,
Where I danced on my tiptoes,
Day and night all so fun,
Rolling in my candy bed,
Friends all welcome in my candy land,
Eating candy day and night,
In my wonderful candy land.

Muhammad Masoom (9)
Nottingham High Infant & Junior School, Nottingham

The Dream

I dreamed a dream in bed last night
Of burgers dancing on giants' heads
And marshmallows raining everywhere
Of giants with pants on their heads
Of invisible Lamborghinis
And no speed limits
To hinder me!

Isa Saleem-Khan (8)
Nottingham High Infant & Junior School, Nottingham

Once I Had A Dream I Was In A Time Ship

Once I had a dream that I was in a time ship
And I was going to take over the world
My first idea was to go back in time and shrink the moon
So everyone would bow to me
And I can change the future
Oh lucky me.

Joshua Maida (9)
Nottingham High Infant & Junior School, Nottingham

I Dream Of...

I dream of a golden window
With fairies peeking out
I dream of devils plotting their evil plans
I dream of knights
Saving princesses
And sometimes, I dream of nothing at all!

Phoebe Forward (9)
Nottingham High Infant & Junior School, Nottingham

If I Were...

If I were a Lego man, and people were chasing me
I wouldn't run away but I would ride a bee
If I were Einstein
Then I would discover a line
Between light and me.

Shlok Sahu Bhansali (9)
Nottingham High Infant & Junior School, Nottingham

Dream

D readful nightmare
R eally happy dreams
E xplore and navigate dreams
A nxious and nervous dreams
M arvellous and magnificent dreams.

Isaac White (9)
Nottingham High Infant & Junior School, Nottingham

Caleb And The Chickens Have An Adventure

When I was making a drink
Baba the chicken told me
'Caleb, there are weird things outside.'
I looked outside and saw nothing
I was very confused
Why was Baba talking to me?
And what was he talking about?
Oliver the chicken came up to me and said
'Caleb, look outside, there are weird things over there.'
I looked out of the window and saw:
A horse that could fly
A red and green striped pig
And a bird with no wings
I was feeling horrified.
Me, Baba, Oliver and Lilly jumped onto the horse's back
And jumped onto Pig's back
And took it in turns to get on the bird's back
And the bird climbed about in the tree
And after that we all had tea
I am glad I found new friends
They are going to have a sleepover.

Caleb Cope (7)
St Peter's Academy, Nottingham

Sweety Town

Down the alley, across the road, up to Sweety Town
'Let's go and find my friend,' I say
'Let's go and find my friend.'

Marvellous Marshmallow Mark
Come out of Doughnut Hall
Sprinkle up your sherbet tie
And let's go out to play

Look at the waving Haribo tree
And the mountain covered in custard
Suddenly Courageous Cookie Clive yelled
'Look out! It's the ice cream!'

Boulders of ice cream were running
Crashing, tumbling down the mountain
Squishing gingerbread houses
Leaving only little crumbs

The town was as flat as a pancake
But we had all survived
We gathered in the old town square
To make our rescue plans

We planted sweets around the town
But they took a while to grow
By the spring the houses grew back
And the town was delicious again.

Oliver Joseph Sherwood (9)
St Peter's Academy, Nottingham

Malteseors In New Yorkie!

I took a trip to New Yorkie, everyone seemed to be porky
The whole place was made of chocolate which seemed a little bit naughty
My friend Megan was with me, we had to move rather quickly
Because the streets were made of chocolate sauce and we were sinking rather swiftly
We spotted a bench made of wafer, and thought it would be a bit safer
If we stayed here for a while, and set off a little bit later
We laid back and gazed at the sky, and saw something flying by
Then there were more, falling to the floor
And people started shouting, 'Oh my!'
One hit the ground and it shook, a man went for a closer look
Suddenly the geezer shouted, 'It's a Malteser!'
And gave it an almighty big suck!
So we thought and we thought of the name...
Malteseors!

Lucy Tomlinson (9)
St Peter's Academy, Nottingham

Elephant Around Bangkok

Cars and traffic is all I can see.
I'm looking for my elephant, can somebody help me?
I'm with my nan,
She's a bit of a gangsta gran.

Bangkok is a big, busy city
Which doesn't help me.
Nan waves for a 'tut tut' and off we go,
I'm looking for my elephant called Jeronimo.

He's big, he's grey,
He must have got in somebody's way!
The traffic is slowing, it's not going fast,
What is the hold up, does anybody know?
We are stuck at the traffic lights
And guess what I can see from the corner of my eye?

Hurray, it's Jeronimo about to walk by.
We get out and run
And Nan jumps up high.
We get on Jeronimo and wave goodbye!

Phoebe Tomlinson (10)
St Peter's Academy, Nottingham

The Play

My mother asked me one day,
'What part did you get in the play?'
My dream would be Cinderella,
With that gorgeous fella,
But my teacher said, 'No way!'

My mother asked me one day,
'What part did you get in the play?'
I dreamed for Gretel
But I got stung by a nettle
So my teacher said, 'No way!'

My mother asked me one day,
'What part did you get in the play?'
My dream was Goldilocks
But I had stinky socks
So my teacher said, 'No way.'

My mother asked me one day,
'What part did you get in the play?'
I got the mean fairy
Cindy says she's hairy
And I push her out the way. Hey!

Yasmin Lyon (9)
St Peter's Academy, Nottingham

Sweet Dreams

I have a dream that is very yummy
It starts as a trip with my mummy
Off we go on a super fast ride
Down a chocolate Curly Wurly slide
We land with a bump on strawberry laces
With big happy grins on our faces
All around us are sweet-filled jars
And rows and rows of candy bars
Mummy says I can fill a big bag to share
With my little brother - it's only fair!
Gobstoppers, bubblegum, cola bottles sour and sweet
Chocolate buttons, space dust
There's so much to eat
I chew the bubblegum and blow the biggest bubble
Pop, it bursts, I need to go or I will be in trouble
Mummy and I float away on a candyfloss cloud
Back to our beds home safe and sound.

Evie McDowell (7)
St Peter's Academy, Nottingham

The Ice Cream House

I'm in a house that is made of ice cream
This is the start of my beautiful dream
My sister's with me inside the house
That's the size of a shed and quiet as a mouse
The windows are made out of fruit-flavoured sweets
And the fridge is bursting with lots of nice treats
The carpet is red and made out of cherries
And the chairs are covered in berries
The yummy cookies cover my bed
Next to my amazing little ted
As we lick more and more of the ice cream
I start waking up from my beautiful dream
I am very sad, the house has melted away
But, I'm happy to start another day.

Ellie Rimmington (7)
St Peter's Academy, Nottingham

Dreams As Big As The Sky

I went to bed and closed my eyes
This is what I saw:
A lion standing on a hill
Doing a big, loud roar

I went to bed and fell asleep
This is what I saw:
A friendly girl bear with a pink tutu
She exclaimed, 'I've got a very strong jaw!'

I went to bed, shut my eyes
This is what I saw:
A massive eagle flying in the sky
Shouting, 'Caw, caw, caw.'

I went to bed and shut my eyes
This is what I saw
All my friends from my previous dreams
Shouting, 'Hooray for our god Thor.'

Amelia Taylor (9)
St Peter's Academy, Nottingham

My Pet Iguana!

My pet iguana is no ordinary iguana
It can sing, it can dance
It can do lots of out of the ordinary things
That a pet can't normally do
We went on an extreme trip to a terrific theme park
On the roller coaster ride he sits in my hood and has a very good time
His spikes are bright pink and his body is a shimmering purple
You may think he is cute but in his mouth are razor-sharp teeth
My iguana is one in a million
He is the best pet in the world!

Amy Clayton (7)
St Peter's Academy, Nottingham

The Penguin Who Danced At Tea

There was a penguin who danced with me,
He swirled and twirled as we were having tea
On an interesting, indigo iceberg,
Floating on a beautiful, blue ocean
With the stars' light,
We dance through the night,
He was a groovy dancer that penguin of mine,
The penguin sang a happy song
As we danced under the moonlight,
I'm sure I saw a whale toss and turn its tail,
Then we went to sleep
With the sound of the crashing sea.

Charlotte King (9)
St Peter's Academy, Nottingham

The Labyrinth

Walls tall, spiders crawl
Monsters lurk and robots smirk
Trying to run, it's not much fun
My friends Daniel and Josh
Have run away and now they're lost
All these creatures are huge
And there's no refuge
Trying to hide in dark spaces
With scared faces
Then a glimpse of light, shining bright
Could this be a way out
Walking forward with no doubt
Let's escape from this maze
Yay! Happy days.

Oscar Middleton (9)
St Peter's Academy, Nottingham

Penguin And Me

Popping bubbles all around
I sit, Penguin and me, on the gigantic, spicy pizza
bobbing up and down
Over swimming unicorns and cities
Around islands full of tiny dinosaurs
Penguin and me, calm and happy as can be
Shoals of people nibble at our pizza
Flying off to islands new
Looking for something, sherbet ice, a polar bed
For Penguin to rest on, and me.

Edward Paling (9)
St Peter's Academy, Nottingham

At Twickenham

There I am
At Twickenham
Standing there with my team
We are all ready and mean
We are against the All Blacks
I can hear the crowd shouting, 'Max!'
I have scored my fifth try
So we may as well say bye
We are the winners
The All Blacks look like beginners!

Max Widdowson (9)
St Peter's Academy, Nottingham

Sport

S wimming, rugby, football and cycling are my games
P reparing to keep fit is my aim
O lympics is where I get my inspiration from
R ugby scrums, football goals, cycling trails, points to be scored, games to be won
T raining to become a sportsman.

Archie William Lever (10)
St Peter's Academy, Nottingham

In Space

Space is as dark as night
The stars are shining like glitter
I am as scared as I would be if I met a dragon
The flying saucers are whizzing by like Usain Bolt
Aliens are wobbling on the surface of the moon like jelly
How am I going to get home...?

Oliver Henshaw (7)
St Peter's Academy, Nottingham

My World

The sun is shining
The wind is blowing
The leaves are rustling
The trees are swaying side to side
Dogs are walking
Sirens are whirring
Can you see the beauty in my world?

George Kennington (9)
St Peter's Academy, Nottingham

My Dream To Mars

I was drifting away and saw some stars
Hoping I'd get to Mars.

When I got there I opened my eyes,
Ate some pies
And saw red everywhere.
When I rubbed my eyes
Everything was dull.

I found a buggy
As clean as can be.
I found my way around
On the scorching red planet
Wishing I could find someone.

I saw something in the distance
I rushed at full speed to see...
It was a Martian!
As green as grass
So I brought him back with me
And brewed some tea
He downed it!
As quick as a pig can find a truffle

I brought him to England
Holding a toy shuttle
I showed him to the world.

And I was famous forever!

Mustafa Khan (9)
Whitemoor Academy, Nottingham

Every Time I Dream It Is Always Different...

Every time I dream, it is always different...
Once I dreamt of a tickling turquoise waterfall, gliding towards the calming, sapphire pool below,
Once I dreamt of a herd of rainbow animals, prancing around,
Like children playing at the park, on the sweet, golden beach at sunset,
Once I dreamt of colourful flowers, reaching high into the heavens, greeting God,
Once I dreamt of an amber sunset, fading into the sea as the glorious blue turns to vicious black,
Once I dreamt of a red river, a glistening ruby ribbon, in a never-ending chase,
Every time I dream, it is always different.

Dominic Curtis (10)
Whitemoor Academy, Nottingham

When I Dream

When I am sad
I dream about glistening water humming the wind's song
Whilst dancing along to the tune like a snake that doesn't dance wrong
I dream about being on the fluffy clouds made of silk
That are a plain-white, like milk
I dream about ponies that are kind and pretty
Jumping up and down like a ribbon of happiness nice and swiftly
I dream about old talking trees that are very happy
But they are a bit wrinkly, they make me laugh.

Niamh Pearce (11)
Whitemoor Academy, Nottingham

Race Car Dream

The race car is as shiny as fire
The race car driver is ready to win the final race in the whole wide world
The race car is as fast as a cheetah and a rocket put together
The race car driver is as flexible as a gymnast
The race car is gold, shiny and has big wheels to go fast
The steering wheel has a lot of grip
So the race car driver does not let his hand slip off.

Hugo Kali (8)
Whitemoor Academy, Nottingham

My Land Of Wonder

I drift away to a land of wonder
It smells of sugary treats
I open my eyes to find a diamond house
With perfume sweets
Underneath my feet I felt and smelled candyfloss
With toffee-buttered popcorn
It smelled like a bakery with all these things to eat
I saw a light like a ribbon
That shone down at me.

Jaylah Clarke (8)
Whitemoor Academy, Nottingham

Untitled

I was lying in the night
There were magical, rich stars
It was like the universe was in the back garden
With peace and quiet, super powers were shooting
A shooting star was coming
Passing through the sleeping stars
Glowing in the dark
There were different coloured stars.

Christine Rutendo Simbi (8)
Whitemoor Academy, Nottingham

The Night

The sun goes down and the world turns black,
That's when we know it's time for bed.
But don't worry, all life isn't dead.
Soon enough the moon will rise
And I, the master of dreams, will admit you into Dreamland.

Inside this world of dreams,
You will see amazing things.
You never know you might grow wings!
When you've grown them you can fly to Mars
And be dazzled by many stars.

Lay down your head upon your bed,
And you can achieve the impossible things,
Only the world of imagination brings.
Once you've entered I shall be your guide,
Because this world is so wide,
And I shall walk you around without limitations,
But with pride.

Remember a beach trip,
A nightmare about getting swept up by the tide,
Beware! But don't be scared,
Because in the world of dreams all is not as it seems...

Sami Rahman (8)
Willow Brook Primary School, Nottingham

Dreams

Let your imagination flow,
Lose reality, fly and grow,
Swirling colours of your mind,
Escape and see what you may find.

Winning medals, scoring goals,
Being the greatest, riches untold,
Running, chasing, being free,
There is no limit of what a dream can be.

Lost in your own private world,
All of your hopes and dreams unfurled,
Anything is possible if you try,
Even wings can grow and pigs can fly!

When you are tucked up in bed,
Thoughts all drifting round your head,
Wonders may carry on through the night,
But be careful of the dreams that bite.

Lilian Robertson (7)
Willow Brook Primary School, Nottingham

Once Upon A Dream

Shopping, baking, holiday's fun.
Dancing and playing in the summer sun.
Dreaming about what our friends say
Dreams explore what we do each day
A cry, a laugh, a nightmare or dream
One makes you laugh,
One makes you scream!
Dreaming of fairies or bright-coloured clowns
Sleeping and dreaming, all peaceful, no frowns
I once dreamed a dream I was lost in the snow
All frightened and cold with nowhere to go
A dream can be happy, a dream can be sad
Dreams of my sisters
Oh, they drive me mad!
I don't always remember all of my dreams
Those that I do, what do they mean?

Rebecca Grace Barks (7)
Willow Brook Primary School, Nottingham

In My Dreams

In my dreams I like to go out walking,
In my dreams I like to walk all day,
In my dreams I like to see the flowers,
Especially in May.

In my dreams I like running through the bushes,
In my dreams I love climbing up the trees,
In my dreams I like to taste the honey
From all those friendly bees.

In my dreams I like to smile,
In my dreams I run a mile,
In my dreams I am swimming in the sea,
In my dreams you are with me.

Katie Limon (8)
Willow Brook Primary School, Nottingham

My Wonderful Dreams

On a Monday I dream of being under water,
On Tuesday I dream of space,
On Wednesday I dream of the fair,
On Thursday I dream of the circus,
On Friday I dream of the beach,
On Saturday I dream of the Olympics,
On Sunday I dream of Germany.

Dreams can be scary, dreams can be nice
I may not always dream but I still enjoy them
Dreams are sometimes true
Even when dreams are scary
I always think of past dreams.

Holly Limon (8)
Willow Brook Primary School, Nottingham

In My Wonderland...

In my wonderland the clouds are made of candyfloss
In my wonderland people never get cross

In my wonderland you can always hear a joyful song
In my wonderland people always get along

In my wonderland fairies flutter by
In my wonderland people lay and watch the sky

In my wonderland you use a unicorn to fly
In my wonderland the impossible is possible...
If you try.

Maisy Gallacher (7)
Willow Brook Primary School, Nottingham

Dreams Can Come True

What is your dream?
Winning the race?
Putting a smile on a special person's face?
Win an Olympic gold?
Never grow old?
Anything is possible if you try

Be a superstar?
Drive your favourite car?
Climb a mountain?
Jump in a fountain?
It really doesn't matter

Just have...
 D etermination
 R esilience
 E ndurance
 A mbition.
 M ake it happen!

Grace Smithies (7)
Willow Brook Primary School, Nottingham

Superhero

Staying at home to fighting crime,
I wish I was a superhero.

Saving the day, cheering my name
Waving a flag
Beating the bad.

Flying up high,
Soaring the sky,
People to save,
I give them a wave.

I hear a shout, it could be Mum,
My time as a superhero is done,
Time to get up and face the day,
I guess saving the world in my dreams,
will have to be OK.

Keira Cullis (9)
Willow Brook Primary School, Nottingham

An Astronaut

You could be flying past the stars,
Just waiting to get to the moon,
Waiting to discover new worlds.

A new world,
Is that Mars chocolatey and sweet?
Or is it the Milky Way filled with delight?
I started to eat a marshmallow.

Suddenly I awake,
Feeling very podged and full
Where has my pillow gone?
I burped and a feather came out.

Harry Whiteley (7)
Willow Brook Primary School, Nottingham

Once Upon A Dream

I was in my bed,
But then I met my dread,
It was a little bat,
But it hurt my head.

I was in the lake,
Using a rake,
Then a crocodile came and said,
'Chomp chomp, I'd like your head.'

I was in the river enjoying my swim,
But had to go home so I said, 'Bye-bye,'
Just before he ate my head.

Charlotte Lucy Mutton (7)
Willow Brook Primary School, Nottingham

Once Upon A Dream

I closed my eyes
And what a surprise
A unicorn flew by
High in the sky
With sparkly wings
Flying through rings
I jumped on his back
And he told me his name was Zack
He flew with his friends
To where the fun never ends
I sat on a cloud
And the unicorns were loud
I suddenly woke up
And lying next to me was my pup.

Ellie Reast (7)
Willow Brook Primary School, Nottingham

Me And My Best Friend

Friends are kind, honest and not cruel,
I meet my best friend at school,
We play all day and have a laugh,
We smile, we cry and both hate maths,
My best friend has an adventurous mind,
Whilst I'm quite quiet, shy and kind,
Two girls together who are never mean,
Me and my best friend make the best team.

Grace Deuchars (7)
Willow Brook Primary School, Nottingham

Kenning Poem

In my dreams I see...
Child-scarers,
Sword-bearers.
Chain-linkers,
Ship-sinkers.
People-killers,
Scary chillers.
Pumpkin-chasers,
Losing-racers.

Grown-up achievers,
School leavers,
Rock song-singers,
Glory-bringers,
Goal-scorers,
World-explorers,
Sith-defeaters,
Strawberry-eaters.

Bertie George Freestone (7)
Willow Brook Primary School, Nottingham

Unicorn Dream

You wish you were a unicorn,
Flying high up in the sky,
Shooting stars up above,
Glittering so bright,
Their horns are so colourful
They are brighter than a star.
They look like a rainbow,
Glittering in the night sky.

Izzy Whiteley (7)
Willow Brook Primary School, Nottingham

I Wish I Could

I wish I could fly,
In the night sky,
I would wave Bessie bye-bye,
I would go so high,
Why would you sigh?

Ollie Holland (7)
Willow Brook Primary School, Nottingham

Young Writers
Est.1991

YOUNG WRITERS INFORMATION

We hope you have enjoyed reading this book – and that you will continue to in the coming years.

If you're a young writer who enjoys reading and creative writing, or the parent of an enthusiastic poet or story writer, do visit our website www.youngwriters.co.uk. Here you will find free competitions, workshops and games, as well as recommended reads, a poetry glossary and our blog.

If you would like to order further copies of this book, or any of our other titles, then please give us a call or visit www.youngwriters.co.uk.

Young Writers
Remus House
Coltsfoot Drive
Peterborough
PE2 9BF
(01733) 890066
info@youngwriters.co.uk